A Boy Named *Boy*

Growing Up Black in "Whitetown"
During the 1960s, Hampstead, NC

Earl S. Braggs

Copyright© 2021 Earl S. Braggs
All rights reserved

ISBN: 978-1-7324369-8-5

Cover Illustration: Joseph V M (pixbay.com)

Wet Cement Press
Berkeley, California

www.wetcementpress.com
wetcementpress@gmail.com

Wet Cement Press publishes small handheld books of poetry, prose and hybrid genius.

WCP9-3

for my daughters

Rashida Kamilah Braggs

and

Anastasiya Elaine Braggs

People have long told long stories like our story, but most never quite as long.

Picture this: A Colored grandmother and five Colored grandsons sitting on the back porch of a little shack situated off-center in the middle of a White town, listening to an afternoon transistor radio, November 22nd 1963, the day John F. Kennedy died. Like so many Colored people back then, we were not afraid to cry at funerals and after-the-funeral were never afraid to fry fish. JFK had been our hope and our hope had died that afternoon in Texas. Later that day, into the woods I remember going, sitting on a tree stump, solitude surrounded by solitude. I wondered as far away as why Miss Brenda, the bookmobile lady, found it so necessary to make sure I knew that starfish disappear at night when stars come out. I wondered if she knew if starfish would still disappear if stars, one night, decided not to shine. Sitting there, still, as a kind of mourning that waits for tears to form,

I waited for a world with no more Camelot to start turning again. I pressed my ears up against a blue wind of questions that tried to answer themselves but couldn't. Echoes rang out as church-service bells, I was not alone. Siddhartha had always followed me everywhere I went. Listening to the patience of trees is a virtue.

We were trash pile children, coming of age in a White-trash pile town.

Days of *Saltlife* grace peppered with nights not quite so carried the weight of our black and white polka dot world.

Whitetown wasn't painted white like a white picket fence, but everything was white-washed white except us. And so it was us and them.

In a fish house town, we lived in a centered-off corner, in front of and behind the psychology of White ways of thinking inside of and outside of a fish box. Many dusks and dawns we witnessed the sun trade places with the moon, never knowing what the next trade-wind day would blow into the making of ends meet that had never met before, but knew each other as old acquaintances. Early morning after early morning the howls of haunting owls reminded us to get up, wash our faces and face the things we already knew, the things White people just didn't talk about back then when Colored people were without or within hearing distance. For psychological comfort, I suppose, White people swallowed the ugly words of one week so that the next week would be nice weather, a be-kind-to-Colored-folks week. Still, most weeks we were aim-straight-down-range people.

Some of the community called my brothers and me amusement-at-the-Pender-County 4H-Club-Fair boys. Many Saturday nights we were defined by design as nothing more than shooting-gallery-arcade people. "Two niggers for a nickel, step right up, try your luck."

We were moving targets that knew which way not to move. I won't say we knew our places, but our places seemed to know us by something other than a Negro named *Boy*. Master mathematicians, we knew how to misrepresent numbers. Like an accountant cooking books, we knew how to cook butter beans, white potatoes with ham hocks, okra over the top and make the combination with a little salt and pepper taste good. Like something hunted, we blended into the environment when we needed to be unnoticed.

The art of figuring out trajectory is a Negro natural science. Too many scientists have paid no attention to the honest implications of living a blacked-out life. Incoming fire, we saw just before stepping to the side, always just in time. Something out of this world or something on the other side of this world told us not to notice how ordinary it was to be on the wrong end of a "bad" aiming dream. It was as if normal nigger things happened only on normal nigger days. Through years of hurricane seasons, good weather, fair weather, hot weather, cold weather, we sidestepped defeat. Every day was as normal as any other normal day. Mosquito protection, we never wore. Bitten by mosquitoes, we seldom were. We knew how to dance around the killing sounds of mosquito songs.

The White people of Whitetown never could figure out the rhythms of our swamp waters playing Negro blues. They never took time to listen long enough to hear the magic. And this, we knew, so naturally we carried our lyrics as weapons of words, normal as any normal day in Hampstead, North Carolina.

Years into the future of my growing up in Whitetown I met a middle-aged White woman who told me a secret. She was in the audience, and I was on stage reading poetry. The audience was still clapping when she approached the podium. "I like what you just read," she said. Between us, a quick exchange. People were starting to wait in line for the book signing. I was scheduled to sign copies of my latest book at the time, *Syntactical Arrangements of a Twisted Wind*. Before she walked away, disappearing into the crowd, she asked if I would like to have breakfast with her the next morning. Conversation over eggs over easy was an epiphany. She lived outside of Omaha, Nebraska. "I'm a Corn Husker," she said. She told me that she worked at a social service agency and only one Black woman worked there with her. She told me the Black woman invited all of her co-workers to come to her church that next Sunday.

"My husband and I were the only ones to go," she said. Sitting comfortably in the pews of an African American Church listening to the sway of a Black choir "Something beautiful was lifted in me that I never knew I had." She was almost crying. We crossed a lot of borders over breakfast that morning. Before we parted, as she was hugging me, she whispered, "Every White family in America should go to a Black church service at least once a year and listen. Only then," she said, "only then, when they listen, will the spirit of America slowly turn into being America the Beautiful." The secret that she told me that morning has remained with me like rabbit-eared pages in a library book that has never been checked out.

The bookmobile came to *Our Town* because we lived in Whitetown. The White lady that drove the bookmobile was always on time, and just in time she taught me to read O. Henry's short stories and Thornton Wilder's performances long before the Pender County Public Library considered Negroes to be "public" enough to check out library books.

Our life was a life of walking and reading telltale signs with caution without being cautious.

We were careful not to incite, careful not to push the pull of a White trigger-happy man getting ready to . . .

But? Some days we didn't even bother to try, we knew there was no way we could be as carelessly careful as the point-blank aim of a rifle with no bullets, laughing, getting ready to get loaded up on some nigger-killing moonshine.

I think I was nine years old when a drunk White man put a gun to my head so he could watch himself laugh at me shaking in the shotgun seat of my uncle Earnest's old Ford truck. My uncle Earnest didn't say a word then, didn't say a word afterwards. Silence is also a virtue.

Every day we stared into our own darkness, a darkness that revealed we had little defense to deflect incoming projectiles of racism. Fear, we saw it coming and going and didn't see it coming or going all at the same time.

Our days were made-up days as if they were theater lines staged for a performance, another small town *Our Town* production of James Baldwin's *Go Tell it on the* [other] *Mountain*.

My oldest brother, Lee, went to Heaven when he was fourteen. I can still see the blown off left shoe left at the scene of the electrocution. That Saturday morning, my Uncle Earnest and Lee had gone looking for copper wire and other scrap metal to sell to the junk man. Lee must've jumped too high to reach the "hot" wire dangling from that telephone/power line pole. As the ambulance pulled away, I knew that was the end of my brother, the end of Lee Anthony's story. Yes, he died later that day, but something inside of me was born that day. Living my life almost as two people, since that day, Lee has lived inside of me. Years later, when I studied Jack Kerouac's *On the Road*, I learned that Kerouac's older brother, Gerard, died of rheumatic fever, age nine. Kerouac said Gerard followed him for the rest of his life as a guardian angel.

I loved Lee, but not as a big brother, more as a younger brother. I could bat better than him, catch better than him. I could run faster than he could. I could hit homerun after homerun, he never hit a baseball that far. Later that day we were supposed to play a baseball game, then go night fishing once it got dark. I wonder now if stars came out that night, I wonder if starfish went in. Then again, I think I know.

We were no-time-out-in-the-game children. Baseball games, we played outside the batter's box. We ran outside of base lines and outside of color lines in ways Negro-simultaneity was never quite able to accurately measure. The 90 feet from home plate to 1st base never equaled the 90 feet from 3rd base to home plate.

"Nigger boy out-racing the speed of a baseball" provoked taunts and jeers deeper than the broken-bat homeruns I blasted over white-washed fences.

We heard but did not hear the White umpire call, "'You're out' side of the line, boy."

When Bobby Midget and his brother Johnny and the rest of the White boys of Whitetown decided to let us dark boys play, I played center field every chance I got. I loved baseball, the thrill of it all. Sliding in headfirst, just missing the tag, I loved stealing 2nd base especially when Johnny was behind home plate trying to throw me out by inches.

And by inches, every time, he almost did, but never could.

We lived, abandoned, in a barn-looking shack overlooking the once over-farmed, worn-out dirt edges of a weed field. We owned no automobile, we walked everywhere we went. Up and down the asphalt roads and dirt paths of any day, we carried everything we could afford to carry in brown paper sacks. Our days were hard, uneven days, disconcerting, yet lovely as peacefulness some days.

We loved the steadfast gaze and unwavering concentration required to walk on railroad track rails because we challenged rails as a matter of balancing White people's advantage against our disadvantage. "The Lord will make a way," Grandmamma Ruth would whisper her homemade honesty against walls of disbelief, against the statues of Stalemate and her good sister, Promise. Renting enough faith to believe that we would not fall, we never fell. Time was supposed to tell, but time never did tell us anything else, so we had to figure it out, one step at a time, walking on rails, pushing forth the everyday needs of wanting and waiting and watching things we could not see like me amounting to anything in life but a "hill of beans."

Improvising, day in and day out, the velocity of nothingness, we channeled hard times in directions away from our hearts.

We were blues music people, people just like that Omaha, Nebraska lady, years later, would describe to me over breakfast. We toted our transistor radio songs like toting a sack of singing sweet potatoes, still warm, brown sugar, lots of butter.

Muted jazz played on top of the blues grew-me-up and out into my growing up years. There was Miles Davis, then John Coltrane bringing forth the birth of coolness. John Lee Hooker, hooked up to an electric guitar. On the same stages stood B.B. King and Miss Bessie Smith re-declassifying the classifications of church-house blues. All of this, divided un-carefully into my twanging nights of Hank Williams and Miss Patsy Cline. Patsy Cline's "Walking after Midnight" and "Crazy" country and western blues knew the best way to not rock me to sleep was to keep singing, keep twanging the night away. Patsy Cline's lyrics, melodies and refrains of sadness did not make me sad. They made me feel her blues beneath the words, made me feel as if she knew what Black people were going through. But it was the rhythm and blues of soul music, Motown, in the morning that rocked and rolled up the torn sleeves of my always-too-short long sleeve shirt sleeves of never quite blending out or blending into the carefully plotted blowing white winds that carried us in spite of intent.

Hampstead, North Carolina, back then was a no stoplight, crossroad town stopping and starting at the neck of the T intersection where State Road 210 ran perpendicular to Highway

17. There were two fish houses. The bigger one, Hampton Jack Lea Fish House was where a stoplight would be, and J.J. Smith Fish House was located less than a country-long-city-block-walk up State Road 210. For years without any loose pocket change, we lived in Hampstead between three Jesuses and the smell of two fish houses. The three Jesuses were Baptist, Methodist and Presbyterian. The three Jesuses all looked the same from the outside looking in, but we knew exactly how to tell each one from the other two.

The fish houses were distinct as the fish house proprietor men, competing to out-fish-smell each other on a daily basis. Prosperity was measured by the shape, size and weight of undressed fish in iced-up fish boxes. The three Jesuses factored, religiously, into profit margins in un-sacred ways not to be articulated in fish house terminology. But everyone understood that a fish-face was the only face on a hundred dollar bill in Hampstead, North Carolina during those days.

In church house yards, in neighborhood yards and all other fish smelling yards, each Jesus took turns teaching the art of scaling and cleaning (some called it dressing) fish. Everyone knew, it seems, from birth that some fish heads you cut off, some fish heads you leave on. The angle of holding a fish knife told us from birth, "equal" does not mean "equal" and that for a Negro, fried fish and grits for breakfast was always the best catch of a good day in Hampstead, North Carolina.

It was Venus flytrap country, a carnivorous swamp town up upon a flatten out fish-top hill, fourteen feet above the level of our sea, the Atlantic Ocean. For a long time I thought we lived below the level of the sea like Black people in New Orleans who buried the dead on top of the ground so the dead would not float away. Our seacoast main road, Highway 17 (the King's Highway, US Route 17) was the last highway on the east coast of our North Carolina blue world. Highway 17 ran from somewhere in upstate Virginia to somewhere in down-state Florida. It ran straight through the middle of Hampstead, separating J. J. Smith from Hampton Jack Lea, separating me and my four dark brothers from three White Hampstead Jesuses.

Growing up African American, Colored, Negro, nigger boy, Black and broke as in no money whatsoever in a White people town during the 1960s, one would think that I did not have a happy childhood. Surely, if one were to look back closely enough to hear the chance-encounter sirens of racial segregation, see the un-put-out-able volunteer fire truck fires of somebody that resembled the idea of Christ begging on a burning cross, smell the "Colored people" smoke of that turbulent history, one would without the smell of doubt conclude without the need to conclude that there was no way any kind of happiness could come out of the thickness of that kind of fire-choking-a-nigger smoke.

Yet, the black and white photographs taken from my growing up years of staring and looking into the lens of somebody's Kodak camera picture me smiling a lot more often than not. My teeth were almost always gleaming white because I brushed and blessed my religious mornings with Arm and Hammer (pure) Baking Soda, the only toothpaste we could afford. I was happy in my baseball card contentment. I had two shoe boxes full. Name a player, I had the card. Willie Mays, Hank "Henry" Aaron, Mickey Mantle, Whitey Ford, Elston Howard (the first Black player to play for the New York Yankees), Roger Maris (hit

61 homeruns in 1961, breaking Babe Ruth's record), Bobby Richardson, Yogi Berra ("Déjà vu all over again"), Joe Pepitone, Roberto Clemente and on and on, two shoe boxes full.

In spite of trying to learn to pronounce the names of odd-named baseball players in those uneven made years, my childhood was a happy childhood. Most days I managed to push my little green plastic toy soldier boys just far enough into the battle zone to win the war. Life was good like a T shirt, I guess, good as it could be by necessity.

Black children, I believe, are born with an innate need to make a shirt that doesn't fit, fit like it was made to fit.

Walking the roads of Hampstead as uninvited as Colored people was an old- tramp-looking-White-man with a long cigarette colored beard. His name was two first names, Joe and Bill. We often saw Joe Bill picking up soda drink bottles and beer cans as we walked from place to place. Strange how he was never going in the same direction we were going. By design, probably not, he was too off-center to know where the center of why was, and I don't think he could see well enough to see what color the fence was painted. Without a notion of anything that was not a drink bottle or a beer can, Joe Bill lived his off-White life in a fish town bucket just like us Colored people.

Joe Bill, ambling announced along Highway 17, toting bottles and cans in a burlap sack, he mattered only to himself. He sold his bottle and can catch of each day to Mr. Kye Howard's grocery store. Somebody said he was related to somebody, but I don't think anybody wanted to be related to Joe Bill. At the store sometimes he would sit on the tall end of a Coke bottle crate and tell war stories and lies. All the years we listened to his stories, he wore the same clothes, winter, fall, spring, summer, a worn-out WWII field jacket and bib overalls.

Joe Bill would always start one story, then stop and start telling another story, never returning to the original story. His way of telling a story always made us laugh, and we loved to laugh back in those days. We needed, so much, to laugh at anything funny enough to make us laugh.

We had no electricity. I don't think the electric lines and telephone lines had any idea that we lived in a house within speaking distance of a line of power utility poles that always seemed to lean in the wrong direction. We had no running cold or hot water, no bathtub bubbles. All we had was just a foot-tub-tin-bucket for taking a once-a-week bath. Usually on Sunday mornings before church, my brothers and I would flip coins to be first. You just can't get clean in dirty water. First hand, this I learned because my brother Tyrone was the real gambler in the family. On cold winter nights, we counted the steps to the outside shithouse. Grandmamma told us not to use that word, but we used that word behind her back every chance we got. In our house there were no books to be read shelved upon the nonexistence of book shelves. Bookmobile books, we stacked in corners so we wouldn't forget when the bookmobile lady would come the next time. We had no faux Persian rugs on soft pine wood floors, no summer ice refrigerator maker, no pantry stock piled with cans of pork n beans or sardines, no plastic bags of dry lima beans and other dry goods, no screened in windows to the dislike of mosquitoes, no red flag wearing mailbox on the side of the road marking where we lived, no letters of hope ever arriving in the mail. Our mail-call life was a General Delivery life. We walked to the post office once a week to pick up mostly nothing. "No mail for Miss Ruth today, sorry. How is she, by the way?" Miss Irene, the mail lady would say. Even the grass in our front yard refused to grow because it didn't seem to know we cared, I guess, like White people cared to take care of their lawns with weed wackers and John Deere riding lawn mow tractors.

Every last word in a book we saw at night was by the dim light of lamplight as long as we had enough kerosene to keep flames flickering.

The only things solid we had to stand upon were Black people magic, Colored people love and the Negro way of singing a spiritual song. We improvised life on an edge, sharp as a dull kitchen butter knife. On bed-bugged mattresses, we slept between the damp dimming blades of *forget* and *forgive*, slept between the winter weather coldness of *I don't know* and *I told you so*, slept between the thin weight of thin blankets and homemade quilts.

Most cold nights, we cuddled up with winter-like hibernation in whatever second-hand clothes we happened to be wearing that day, yesterday and sometimes, the day before yesterday.

Hard times were hard in a soft, almost caring kind of way that somehow didn't seem that hard at all. We never felt that times were hard the way Grandmamma did. Between dips of Railroad Mill and Navy snuff, she would spit small, brown puddles and say, "Lord, these times are tough." We never felt how tough times were. Without concerted notice, I guess we were born with the ability to step over the rough edges of tough times.

Christmas cards didn't know where we lived. But always, we had a beautiful Christmas tree decorated with mostly nothing but red holly berry twigs. Our shack, unhandsome as she was, sat surrounded by beautiful pine Christmas tree woods. So simple it was to bring an axe or a handsaw along on a late November or early December morning.

Almost never did we get anything for Christmas except for that one time when a White family (I forget their name, they were relatively new residents, from up North somewhere) gave the five of us boys a red and blue bicycle. The twins were too young to ride, so it was just us three and we didn't care that it was a girls bicycle. It wasn't new, but it rode like it was Sears and Roebuck brand spanking new, right off of the showroom floor of the catalog store. It was very late November, so I guess that counts as an early Christmas present.

So simple it was to take a Sagittarian walk through the astrological reasons we celebrated our being without proper consent to be born under any zodiac sign. There were never any birthday parties in our house, no birthday cards, no birthday presents, no "Happy Birthday" to any one of us five Black boys growing up avoiding the thorns of rose bushes that grew wild like wild blueberry bushes. Hampstead was surrounded by blueberry fields forever.

I loved the bookmobile lady, and she loved the inquisitive mind of me. Waiting for her was my great war of anticipation, testing the patience of trees. Some days she would let me ride with her part-way around her route. White kids waiting for bookmobile stories to be told were envious of me not because I was a Colored boy standing in the Do Not Stand Here spot next to the driver's seat, but because she was pretty like a *Look* magazine picture of Elizabeth Taylor. Flipping through musty bookmobile library books, many nights, stories upon stories upon plays told themselves to me. I bookmarked pages I loved listening to, I bookmarked pages I couldn't wait to hear, I bookmarked page after page, the sounds of poverty reading poetry. The math and science books of our sociology years were always left open to the disordered pages of another war story told before it should be told. Told like a Joe Bill story, but that's another story. So this, now, is the story of another war story told before it should be told.

I was born a centaur, delivered by a White doctor working his Colored people shift at a Black hospital, Community Hospital, Wilmington, North Carolina. The first birthday cake I cut that was designed and decorated to celebrate me was at a bash thrown on the day I turned twenty-one. Six months earlier, I had landed on foreign soil, Clark Air Force Base, Angeles City, Republic of the Philippines, Southeast Asia. I was stationed within smelling distance of South Vietnam, and I could smell the smell of what smelled like the rotting smell of rotten fish and rice burning. During those years, I was smoking too much pot to accurately plot the course that led my decisions in the dazed directions that they took, unnoticed. But in that unnoticing haze tied together by Thai sticks of pure THC, I did notice that I was not among the ones who smoked heroin-laced cigarettes at work and nodded off while sitting on the toilet. Our sergeant had to have known. In a way it was funny, you would just walk into the latrine and they would be sitting there nodding, stall door wide open, the ashes of a complete cigarette burned down to the filter, still holding onto its dead heroin-laced cigarette life.

During those dead zone years, dead zone cities and small towns sent each of us as far away from home as possible, then gave each of us permission to tell our own personal growing-up war stories and how they blended into moments and minutes of being a soldier in a death count zone. We were the casualties of our war stories. Talking with the Brothers I hung out with, I realized that our stories mirrored each other's, but none, if any could add the elements of my experience growing up in a White town. I guess it made me see the world in black and white and in "White." Every lesson taught is not every lesson learned, but I learned enough from the "White" side of my life to know that among the White boys and girls I grew up with none was smarter than me, none could play baseball better than me and not one of them could look me in the eyes and say, "I'm superior to you because I am White." Circumstances raised me to know better. Joe Bill told his stories out of sequence because life is out of sequence. Growing up, realizing first hand that the notion of White superiority was manufactured to look like it was real when it was so far from the truth, I could smell it a country mile away. Most of the African Americans I went to high school with and served in the Air force with struggled to see racism in the way I was pretty much born to see it. White superiority is like faux fur. It's lauded as long as African Americans fail to realize that it's a fake and baseless claim. I have always wondered what real foxes think of faux foxes.

It amazes me, even now, that I remember what I was remembering, standing in front of my first birthday cake, surrounded by Air Force green work uniforms, about to cut into the fact that I had made it to my twenty-first birthday. I remembered my battles to play on the White Methodist baseball team, the verbal skirmishes of working at the fish house blues, the conflicts of my interest in White girls as girlfriends, the tiffs and squabbles of dirt-poor-rent-free life, but mostly I remembered cities of war and war torn high school years. My high school hallways were hallways on fire, navigated by the wearing of black or white, high top or low top Chuck Taylor tennis shoes. All basketball games, canceled. Classrooms of smoke-laden intentions disguised as themselves didn't fool any one of us. All after school activities, canceled. Conflicted pages unread, adding fuel to the flames.

All things not mentioned, canceled. The oxygen of race war, the only air pure enough to breathe. A race war car in the parking lot, parked in the principle's parking spot. NAACP buses parked next to school buses. The school buses, neither of which wanted to figure out the abbreviations formed from the initial letters of "other words" used to define and describe us. So in other words, that one day, my cousin, Ronnie was defined by and disguised as a loaded gun.

Ronnie attended New Hanover High School, I was at John T. Hoggard High. That day of cancellations during that raggedy riot-torn semester, Ronnie, Grandmamma Ruth's sister's daughter's son, brought a concealed weapon to my classroom, but waited until lunch to give it to me in the cafeteria. Lunch time was a bad car wreck on the runway that day. I am sure Siddhartha was there somewhere, but he was nowhere to be seen. Cafeteria chairs had no patience for sitting down and being quiet. Lunch trays were flying into the faces of White boys. Black afro sisters and cornrow hair girls were flying up and down the hallways, dragging White girls by their blond ponytails. The New Hanover County Sheriff Department White patrol officers were handcuffing and arresting only Black boys and girls. Armed, concealed, dangerous and scared, I ran all the way home through the woods. When I got home, the WECT News was already on the television. Watching the depiction, I posed to myself this question: Was I fighting to learn or was I learning to fight? I have never been quite sure which one carries the weight of the whole truth and nothing but... Anyway, without realizing the complicated implications of it all, I turned and doo-wopped, "...eighteen with a bullet," just as the song lyrics say, "got my finger on the trigger, I'm gonna pull it."

A race riot war was raging in the streets of Wilmington, North Carolina. In our un-celebratory stances, we were dancing the Charleston (SC) with red bricks, heavy in our hands, ready to break the backlog of downtown storefront windows of discrimination. And there I was, a political prisoner of another undeclared war burning in my own schoolyard, my own backyard. I remember the National Guard tanks rolling through Jervay Projects, cutting tank track marks, horizontal, into the concrete of our front lawn sidewalks. I can still taste and smell the putrid smoke of teargas dropped by National Guard helicopters hovering over our living-in-the-red-brick projects backyard clotheslines.

I was six months from turning nineteen when my nineteenth birthday looked back and saw me, face down in the grass, caught in a blood-red crossed-up crossfire between the Wilmington Police Department and the Wilmington Ten. The Wilmington, North Carolina race riots of 1971 engulfed the city like the rage of a California wild fire.

We didn't know who was what, but the Police Department's bullets knew their targets very well. It was late that Saturday night. Our section, the Black section of town was under a 9 p.m. curfew. It was beyond hot that late June late evening news day. We wanted some KFC. It was 10 p.m. We were teenagers. We were hungry, hungry for the smell of some good ole Southern fried chicken with brown gravy poured across the unlidded top of a Styrofoam cup packed with KFC mashed potatoes.

The piercing sounds of bullets flying back and forth above your head, bullets coming from every which of a way is like a jazz solo in a way because all you really hear at that moment is trumpet music coming forth to carry you home. The police were set up behind make-shift barricades in front of KFC, closed for business that night. We should have known, but as I said, we were teenage boys, Saturday-night hungry. Across Dawson Street, under the cover of Hill Crest Housing Projects, some Black boys, the authorities later claimed to be members of the Wilmington Ten, were returning fire from around red brick housing projects corners. Between the two extremes, we were trapped in the itching nose science of un-freshly mowed grass, faces down, buried, with the backs of our heads looking up into the reaches of an unlovely night city skyline that forgot to hang the crescent shape of a fisherman's moon, that forgot to be kind as it had been even during thunderstorms and hunting season when White, good ole boys shot deer and "coon" with hunting rifles. Nothing prepared me to be in the middle of what became a national crisis on evening news television sets watching reflections of themselves sitting on couches in living rooms in every city in America.

The Wilmington Ten were 9 Black boys I went to school with and a White woman from somewhere in Ohio, I believe. Jerry Jacobs, my cousin, and Willie Earl Vereen, one of my best friends, and Joe Wright, the "Lying Philosopher," were the three of the Ten that I was closest to. Another of the Ten, Connie T., a boy I didn't like at all. How could I? Connie

T. knocked me out on purpose, the first play of the Turkey Bowl football game that year. I saw him break across the line, buckling eyes with me. Bam! Lights out. Why did he hit me so hard, I wasn't even carrying the fucking football? I woke up on the sideline.

Someone (I never found out who) tied a red Jimi Hendrix bandana around my head to keep my brains from falling out, I guess. The Turkey Bowl tradition went way back into the '50s, pitted ex-convicts and felons against those of us who had not yet been lucky enough to have been to jail or prison. In Jervay Projects during those days it was an honor to go to prison and come back up to the corner to brag about it. On that same corner, showing off, JB Cooper put a gun to my head and told me to get down on my knees and pray. I didn't get down on my knees, I didn't pray and I didn't say please. I believe JB and Connie T. were sent to training school when they were sixteen or seventeen, so they qualified, plus Connie T. was about 6'3", 250 lbs., the tallest and biggest of the "Accused."

According to the *Wilmington Star*, the Wilmington Ten were wrongfully convicted in 1971 of firebombing (arson) and conspiracy. Sentenced to 29 years in prison, most served almost a decade before appeal won their release. The Wilmington Ten, they were the ones of true valor. The ones of us not brave enough to return fire those days were drafted into the United States Armed Forces. Our rage got the city's attention, the nation's attention, Russia's attention, President Richard Milhous Nixon's attention. The President personally drafted me and all of us. My draft registration was solid as a brick thrown through the window of a White-owned business, which I never did, but I am a witness before and after the fact. My draft registration number was number 1. There was no way in hell I was not going to be sent to Vietnam to kill yellow people. "No Vietcong ever called me a nigger," Muhammad Ali so pointedly pointed out to the Supreme Court of the United States. Vietnam bound, I was, but at the last minute, one or all three of my three Jesuses stepped in and told the United States Air Force to type up orders for Airman Edward Earl Sherman Braggs II, SSN ...-86-0... to be shipped out from Pope AFB, Fort Bragg, North Carolina to the Clark AFB, Angeles City, Republic of Philippines.

Thus, I turned twenty-one with a government-issued gun. My uniform was U.S. Air Force blue, and the girls said they liked the way it fit, as if it was made for me. Made for me, an Air Force blue suit designed by *My Country Tears of Thee*, wrapped in "race" colored construction paper, wrapped un-nicely for me and all of us. In 1972 the President of the United States of America decided without saying loud enough to be heard, "If them niggers want to riot, fight, loot and burn, I'll send them niggers by the slave ship load to South Vietnam, let them niggers fight for their country which, in my Presidential opinion, is not their country at all." No, President Richard Milhous Nixon didn't say this exactly, but that's exactly what President Richard "Tricky Dick" Nixon did. Many of us ended up in Vietnam. But I was lucky, I guess, I ended up slow dancing with a Filipino girl named Cora Castro, celebrating my 21st birthday Southeast Asian style. All the while, then as well as now, I drifted and drift into remembering that Joe Bill told his stories out of sequence because life is out of sequence. So it was the story of an unkind natured backdrop, my personal war on poverty, misinterpreted (on purpose) Separate But Equal educational opportunities for me and my lessons in tragedy that pulled the curtains back, revealing why I couldn't believe a White Master Sergeant in the United States Air Force, Sergeant Fargey, would gather together my friends, my comrades in celebration of a Private Nobody like me. Twenty-one years old, my first birthday present ever, a Swiss army knife. Overcome by 21 years of spared tears, I remembered the sheathed Bowie knife I treasured as a kid. In my moments of under-my-breath contemplation, I revisited the trash pile where I found a White somebody's mistake of throwing Jim Bowie into a garbage-colored trash can. The patience of trees told me to cry, but I didn't. I was a soldier boy, and soldier boys don't cry.

Bare necessity, herself, is the story of continuation. She dictated the rhyme and the reason why Joe Bill's stories never failed to make me laugh, and trash pile life never failed to heap upon me the treasure and excitement of finding stuff and things unclaimed. Looking back, I realize that I needed all the treasures I could find. Growing up, we had no trick-no-treat Halloweens. For Easter we got no new Easter suits for Easter Sunday morning church services. We had no barbeque grill to grill our Independence Day into the evening of the 4th of July. But we always had fire crackers to pop the night away on New Year's Eve. I believe we always knew that the only thing we had to celebrate was the notion of being without, the beautiful side of poverty. Growing up Black in Whitetown, we lived our saltwater music life, dancing while sliding off the side of the moon, the Negro side of the moon. We were the poverty of unread poetry. Somehow, most days, everything seemed to rhyme with whatever time of day our wind-up time clock decided to say. So much of the time our wind-up time clock was wrong because Daylight Saving Time had not been invented yet, and besides Daylight Saving Time doesn't really save time, but we didn't know that back then.

We were trash pile children, *Saltlife* kids. We worshipped the movement of sound waters surfing in from the sea. We honored the coming-in and the going-out of tide levels which we would calculate by sticking a stick down into sound sand and watching for the direction of flow. Besides the murky sounds of sound waters, we depended on nothing else so heavenly. Daily we looked for mermaids beautiful enough to smile approvingly upon us and seahorses large enough to saddle up and ride across waves of forgiveness. Indian names I gave to tide pools and sea brook trees cut by the shape of blowing sea breeze. Names like Tide Moon and Sea That Speaks made the Native American burial grounds upon which we lived seem to come alive and dance to Indian drum beats, beating the U.S. history book account of Native American history until it rained the truth. We were *Saltlife* kids, happy to be up to our knees in salt marsh, jigging for the flat face of a floundering fish big enough for supper.

One time the Pender County Welfare Department tried to give us some welfare food. Welfare food, a whole chicken in a can. We used that whole chicken in a can for pellet rifle-gun target practice. We would shoot it full of holes 'til all of the chicken juice spilled out, then we would open the can and feed welfare chicken to the dog. Some days as we walked along Highway 17, Camp Lejeune Marine trucks would toss out to us C-ration cans of potted sliced steak meat, mashed potatoes and mixed fruit. Soldier boys were better fed than welfare boys. As if we were pioneers, sometimes we carried C-ration cans as we trampled through the wild west of our backyard woods. In the kind thoughts of briers and thickets, we grew up between weeds, dense along the banks of brooks of fresh running brook water. Backwoods kids, we grew up curved, crooked and straight as if we were a part of the forest, the weeds, streams, fords, swamps, cypress tree knots. Holy Christmas we worshipped as tree bush triangles. Curtsied, we did to the queens of honey bees and stinging yellow jackets. We walked with our bare feet touching the earth as often as we could. We celebrated sunlight in a memorial struggle to find sanity in our Negro poverty. Yes, we were happy because one of our three Jesuses allowed us to live close enough to the sea to hear the sounds of ocean waves fighting for space enough to wave at us every day. Ocean waves echoed long like night trains wailing into our long, lonely nights of being the dirt poorest people we knew. Honest to God, I grew up believing we were the dirt poorest people in the world.

We had no bank account, had no under-the-mattress money or extra money. There was no barbershop quartet that would sing around our heads every two weeks or so. We grew afros, beautiful uncombed afros, nappy like un-dreaded locks reaching down upon our front porch no-night-lite softness buried in the hard life of our explored, unrefined happiness. Happy we were because we figured out how to recycle our sad moments so we wouldn't have to invent a new kind of sadness each and every day the Good Lord decided to send through the front and the back doors of our dilapidated-shack lifestyle. We counted our blessing, then multiplied them without ever knowing the psychology of such.

Yes and yes again, we were happy by definitions invented. We were happy because we loved Mr. Rubin, the Jewish traveling shoe salesman. He never failed to knock on our door, unannounced, to check the wear and tear of our shoes. The trunk of his car would always be full as if our stop was the first stop on his shoe route to heaven because he would always preach Grandmamma into buying, mostly on credit, shoes for each of us. I know she must have, but I don't remember her ever buying a pair of pretty shoes for herself. New shoes find it hard to fit feet that walked bare every chance they got. Then again, we were always happy to just look at our pairs of new shoes. On top of the shoe boxes, our shoes looked good while they waited patiently as the patience of trees for the beginning of a new school year to start wearing their soles away.

Every kind of fish loved us because we loved every kind of fish the Fish-Maker could name, and we lived, quite convincingly, between a two-fish-house blues song that never grew tired of singing to us. Both fish houses were within walking distance of the sea. Clams and mussels and crabs and shrimp we loved prepared anyway one could name. Eel we hated because we did not like sea swamp-fed snakes, but some summer nights we cornmeal-breaded eel and fried her up anyway, fried that ugly girl up hard enough to make her taste like a crustacean delicacy. Our happiness answered the question of knowing how to shoot sparrow birds for breakfast and squirrel for lunch, never did know the meaning of brunch. Cottontail rabbit graced our supper table for more dinners than I care to count. Quail were smart, they seemed to always hear us coming long before we saw them flutter away. Shotgun shells scattered through the air, some days we were lucky enough to have quail stuffed with crab meat and gravy over grits for special occasions like every occasion when we had food on our three-good-legs kitchen table. We never had enough food in the kitchen, but we never went anywhere hungry. "The Lord will always make a way," Grandmamma used to say. Grandmamma Ruth was a prophet. She always told us that things would get better. But "better" is not a hard prediction to predict when "better" is measured in measurements less than inches. "Snakes don't eat no grapes," I can still hear myself say when Grandmamma warned me to look out for snakes as we picked wild grapes from the grape arbors that grew along the railroad tracks that ran behind the White people's houses of Hampstead, North Carolina.

Joe Bill would always be walking, picking up bottle and can, then stopping long enough to tell stories long enough to make us laugh. So happiness did indeed live with us in our four-ugly-room shack set back off of Factory Landing Road by almost 75 dirt road-rut yards. Our soft-set-back, never complaining shack outside walls were weathered beyond faded, bad-weather-wind-swept-away gray. Inside of our little propped-up-by-cinder-blocks shack, dead tired walls covered themselves and the cracks of the night and the cracks of the day with daily news newspaper advertisement wallpaper. I remember reading the *Sales* pages of what was on sale at J. C. Penny. I remember the automobile ads, every automobile in the world crammed at the bottom of a page plastered by a thin layer of all-purpose flour mixed with a little water, then glued up onto the wall overlooking the foot of our bed. I knew exactly the kind of cars I wanted when I grew up, a Ford Thunderbird with a ragtop and a red and white Chevrolet Bel Air with baby moon hub caps and four on the floor.

Though Lee later moved to sleep on the floor in the other room, the three of us older boys slept in one bed pushed tight up against one wall and the twins slept with Grandmamma, tight up against the other wall, all in the same room. In our pitiful, little living room where we lived our Nobody-Wants-To-Live-Here life sat a Buddha belly, wood burning, 1912 styled, pre-prohibition potbelly stove that emanated not enough heat in wintertime, but more than enough love all of the time. We loved listening to ghost stories while sitting around the kind flames of Buddha's belly flaring as best he could. Grandmamma called ghosts "hants." We loved Grandmamma Ruth's spiritual, soft, sweet, Southern Negro voice echoing of an evening, slowly vibrating, ever so slightly, the walls of our shack. Rent free, the White owners let us live there for free. Rent free shack, rent free for me, a Negro who had, at that time, no need to know the psychology of such. Rent free. Miss Lillian's mother, an old White lady with a lot of money, let us live there without having to pay her one thin dime. Rent free. All I remember understanding about that kind of rent freedom at that age was that God and all three of our Baptist, Methodist and Presbyterian Jesuses must've liked each one of us a terrible, awful lot.

I did not always live there in the middle of a weed field in the middle of Hampstead in that rent free shack. When I was younger than two years old, Grandmamma Ruth adopted just me and we lived in a different rent free shack located on the very edge of Hampstead. This rent free shack looked like a one story, one tiny room barn with a carport as big as the living quarters. The Methodist Jesus (Miss Cora Mae and Mr. Johnny, the owners, were devout Methodists) allowed for it to be situated underneath the George Washington live oak tree. Rent free life beneath a kind and considerate oak tree, caught red handed in poverty, though I did not recognize it at the time, was a blessing disguised by Spanish moss that knew exactly how to spell my Native American name, Dark Boy with Indian Eyes. There on the edge of Highway 17, I played red-Indian boy against white cowboys. All alone, all by myself beneath my George Washington oak tree, I must have thought that I was Crazy Horse's cousin, must've thought I shot down General George Armstrong Custer. All alone, fifteen definitions of me riding in on fifteen Appaloosas, all arrowheads pointed towards the Battle of Little Big Horn. All alone. The twins, Alphonso and Alonzo, were yet to arrive into the beautiful turmoil of living rent free, and Lee and Tyrone lived elsewhere. Lee was a beautiful, easy going, quiet, angelic boy. Tyrone was a "bad" boy. During the later years when we were all living under one roof, Grandmamma never beat Lee or me, but she had to beat Tyrone with a tree switch, it seems, at least twice a week. Lee, the oldest brother, lived with Mama's uncle on her mother's side, Uncle Buddy. Uncle Buddy lived in Scott's Hill, another little railroad-track, black-community along Highway 17, closer to Wilmington. Tyrone, two years younger than me, lived on the edge of Browntown with another of Mama's uncles on her mother's side, my favorite, Uncle Morris. Uncle Morris was a WWII POW. He couldn't tell you if he was captured by the Germans or the Japanese. He wasn't quite "right" in the head, but I loved Uncle Morris Nixon. As life would have it, my mother fell in love with bright lights and ran away to New York City (the second time) and my father couldn't take care of us by himself. So the arrangement maker arranged it so all the love of a grandmamma and a live oak tree was poured unfiltered upon me and my Siddhartha way of listening to the patience of trees. There on the rest stop side of the King's Highway, in the loose grips of a rent free shack life, Grandmamma and I lived until I started 1st grade at seven years old. My days outnumbered my nights all of those years.

My George Washington live oak tree was located almost on the colorline separating

Hampstead (Whitetown) from the Colored town of Browntown. Rumor has it that my great-great grandmother, Caroline Brown, a midwife, earned enough money to purchase the land and had her sons, all carpenters, layout and build Browntown. Browntown was a worshipped, beautiful Colored community town located approximately one country mile south of my George Washington oak. At the time I was the only Black kid that lived on the White side of that divided by the color of wind world. I was the only kid who could blow, unhurriedly and hurriedly, back and forth across the line without anyone noticing the slightest change in race-measured barometric pressure. Living there in that divided place wasn't as bad as it looked. For reasons out of sequence, sometimes when it rains, it doesn't pour.

Season after season changed, normal as seasons do. Some winters were kind, but summers never were. Bedbugs and mosquitoes, wasps and yellow jackets, black flies and biting yellow flies, spiders and stinging ants, they all loved our open-air-shack-forced hospitality. Snakes cancelled out rats and king snakes cancelled out other snakes and we crossed out calendar days one day at a time. So there beneath my oak tree in a one room shack, Grandmamma and I lived through hurricane season after hurricane season. Hurricane winds were never nice, but I can't remember ever being afraid of the pounding patches of wind and rain pushing against the front door of our little shack. Our one un-boarded up window didn't look strong, but I guess it was determined enough to defeat the elements as long as we were there. Rent free, Grandmamma, me and my George Washington live oak tree survived the bad weather cruelty of poverty. As young as I was, I remember noticing the pure aesthetic beauty of thunderstorms. To this day, I love the sound of hard rain beating down upon a tin roof.

I loved that oak tree, and he, George Washington, loved me. Many summer and warm fall days, I played and slept beneath his pushed out branches. So soundly I would fall asleep as if I owned that tiny part of my Hampstead world. Perfectly placed as a roadside rest stop, my oak tree was inviting. From beneath the shade of kind limbs, I remember the Goatman with his dumb-bell-jingle-bell, broken down, weathered wood cart pulled by two goats. I can see him now, pulling into my beside-the-road-oak-tree-rest-stop, stopping, smoking a cigarette, talking to himself, but never saying a word to me or to my George Washington oak tree. I remember, too, how the two black and white goats seemed to like looking at me. I can also see, still, numerous and countless family vacation packages pulling in and out of the shady spots beneath George Washington's welcoming branches. Woodside two-tone American-made station wagons routinely cruised to a stop. Ford and Chevrolet, Dodge and De Soto ruled the American vacation highways back then. All makes and models of cars and people, packed with vacation stuff and loud kids would pull in, park in the shade to steal needed rest breaks. They would always say hello and goodbye after having a picnic lunch under the Southern hospitable branches of my George Washington live oak tree.

And then there was that day the Gypsies came to get me. I was four or maybe I was five when they came to kidnap me and the shirt right off my back. Routinely, I was just sitting there, looking out from beneath the branches of my oak tree. I saw the green Chrysler car coming before the green Chrysler car pulled in, but Gypsy Rose Lee saw me before I saw her staring out from the most hypnotizingly beautiful eyes I think I have ever seen. With the passenger side door open, Gypsy Rose Lee called clear as my name, "Come to Mama, my dear dark beautiful one, come here, son." I remember her over-red, red lipstick. I remember how large and silver her hoop earrings were and how untangled they were against her almost blue-black, long, straight, Elvis Presley colored hair. I remember her fingers, long; her fingernails, red; her almost soft Gypsy lady voice, "Come here, son." I remember the color of the candy wrapper she offered to me. I remember how sweet, the tone of her inflections and how the soft-softness blended into the evenness of that late morning without being forced, "Come here, son." I remember the husband, eyes straight ahead like driving a Gypsy taxi cab. There were three young, pretty girls in the backseat of a long, snapbean green Chrysler car. I remember the sad brightness in the youngest child's eyes. I remember how beautifully poor the children all were, dressed in so many Gypsy rich colors.

I reached for the Gypsy lady's hand as the wind spoke, Grandmamma Ruth's alerted voice, "No." Off the edge of a cliff, into the front seat of a green Chrysler car, I almost stepped. Where would I be now if...? What Gypsy name would they have given me if...? Would the youngest of the backseat Gypsy girls have smiled if...? Would the sweetness of my chocolate candy colored skin have melted if...? "No, no!" The speed of sound stopped, then started as a gale force breeze left behind by the pace of leaving out words. That snapbean green Chrysler car which was actually a snapbean green Buick Riviera was out of sight in no time flat. Burnt rubber tire marks on the pavement of Highway 17, the only witness. George Washington kept the Delaware River from overflowing again that day. General George Washington leading a column of Continental Army troops saved me as he always did.

According to the history note takers and talkers, part of President George Washington's Southern Journey in 1791 took him from New Bern, North Carolina to Wilmington, North Carolina. Along the way, it is said that Washington and his men had dinner and rested a spell under a live oak tree in the area that today is known as Hampstead. In patriotic commemoration, a granite tree marker was placed beneath my George Washington oak on November 24th, 1925 by the Daughters of the American Revolution. Stretched out beneath a tin roof that was almost touched by far reaching branches, some nights I thought I heard the Daughters out there talking in the dark as I counted sheep leaping across the sky just before falling asleep in a bed of George Washington live oak tree leaves.

When I started 1st grade, I said goodbye to George Washington. George Washington didn't say much to me, but I could tell he was going to miss me trying to persuade him to always be shady, even in winter. I moved to the city. Siddhartha was ready to go as soon as I was. Grandmamma packed me up and took me to live in Wilmington, 17 miles south of Hampstead. We waited kindly as the patience of trees. It was almost 1 o'clock when the 12 o'clock bus arrived. I remember because it was so hot you could see Mojave Desert heatwaves floating across the North Carolina asphalt. I could have fried an egg, if I had had one. The Sea Shore Bus Line only took 30 minutes to change me from a country boy who didn't like to wear shoes to a city boy wearing penny loafers that were too tight, already. City life. That first night, standing beneath the street lights of a city, it was so hard to notice stars and the moon. They weren't happy, I wasn't happy, but there I lived with my mom, dad and brothers in a red brick housing projects home designed for Colored people to remain poor forever. Yet, I thought I was living life like I imagined a rich White kid lived. Yes, I thought I was living the hi-life, living in a red brick house. Mom and Dad rented an apartment in Jervay Projects where my Grandmamma Rosa Bell and Mama's sister, Frances, already lived. Jervay had the reputation of being the "baddest" housing development in the city. Every weekend somebody shot somebody, every month somebody killed somebody, every day somebody swindled somebody out of something else. Every White newspaper carried the Bad Nigger News, religiously, as if it was good-rating news for the 6 o'clock television news. One day Mama sent me to the bakery to get something sweet. I paid for my sweet purchase and dropped the change into a brown paper sack with the purchase. As soon as I stepped out of the bakery door, a boy bigger than me said, "Gee-me that money or I will kill you." I said I didn't have any money. He searched my pockets two times before he walked away. Jervay Place, the "baddest" place in town. For three years, that reputation solidified in my mind. A country-mile boy walking city blocks, lost in the city lights of living a "projects life." Jervay Place, where I learned how to throw a football. Jervay Place, where I had to learn how to fight real cowboys and Indians. Jervay, where I almost got tagged out trying to steal second base from a downtown Jewish-owned "We sell only Colored people church clothes and other accessories" Store. No one was looking, so I detached a plated gold crucifix from a small box, put it in my pocket, thought about my grandmamma, took it out of my pocket, put it back, walked out of Finkelstein's empty handed, feeling I was worth a lot more than the worth of what I did not steal.

City life was a rough-love life if you loved anything about it, which I didn't. I didn't even like my 1st, 2nd and 3rd grade teachers. This I know now because I have no idea what their names were. All I know is I got lost the first day of school and I stayed lost, mostly, for three years. City life was a battle zone and I have a real hit-by-a-rock-in-the-center-of-my-forehead scar to prove how I was awarded my first Purple Heart, a neat little battle wound right between my eyes. One inch left or right would've cost an eye. "You were born lucky," my city-life Grandmamma Rosa Bell said. To this day, I believe what she said that day. Grandmamma Rosa Bell worked as the "Help" for the Chancellor of the local College. She kept her Projects home spotless, plastic over couches and living room chairs. When I graduated from High School at nineteen, she gave me a new white shirt. "This one is like the ones yo daddy used to wear," holding my hand she said. Daddy had been dead less than two months, but I did not cry, I smiled. When my grandmother, Rosa Bell died, I inherited her framed picture of President John F. Kennedy.

The battle zones were outside and inside. Sooner than soon, a street-night moon marked the time when Mom and Dad decided that the morning sun was no longer willing to shine equally upon the both of them. They both had movie star eyes and needed room to shine. Mom went right out into a daylight that felt like night and ended up on a whistling train bound, again, for New York City. It took Mama nine years to get there, live there, return from there. Dad went left and ended up drunk for the rest of his short life. My mother never told me she loved me, yet I know she did. My father told me every day. Yes, I loved my father and he loved me, his namesake. He was and will always be my only super hero. Superman, Batman, I never needed. I later realized that I also loved my mother beyond her movie star eyes and cloudless nights but not before the rains came did I come to understand the implied nature of my mother's kind of bright light, New York City, separated-for-reasons-never-articulated love. When my mother returned from New York, as I said nine years later, she brought with her a son named Lee, another Lee to not replace, but to add to my dear dead brother Lee. Baby boy Lee grew up to look a lot like me. I look just like my father. Maybe there is a missing chapter in that nine year story of my mother and father. Maybe, quietly her love hid from me beneath the church hats she wore. My mother wore beautiful, elaborate hats even on non-hat wearing days. She kept her hats in fancy hatboxes. She called her hats crowns. Many of our Browntown relatives called my mother Queen.

My red-brick-projects days came to a kind but ugly end. I was in the 3rd grade. My brothers and I were taken in by Grandmamma Ruth. We moved to the larger, nicer shack in Hampstead close enough to the ocean to smell her breeze, taste her catch of the day, wear her salt water smiles upon my face. Down the road a bit from the middle of Whitetown, I lived in beautiful poverty until at sixteen I was kicked out of the Pender County School System for inciting a riot that I did not invent.

Hampstead, North Carolina, typical in those days, a still-angry-that-the-South-lost-the-Civil War, unincorporated, small town that smelled of fish from January to December. Hampstead, North Carolina, a hurricane wind-blown town with three Jesuses and three nicely kept cemeteries placed far enough away from each other so that the respective ghosts had proper roaming distance without running into each other, rekindling some kind of religious feud that was buried years ago either over here or over there. Hampstead, North Carolina was racist, typical as I said, yet in many ways it was Heaven sent. It saved us from city poverty. City-life poverty is rats and roaches and street crime and not having enough of anything truly needed; whereas country-life poverty is a kind, soft "not having" because everything around you provides. Country-life gives. City-life steals from its own city poverty. Country-life affords what it takes. Living in the country, we were so poor we had no roaches and that didn't have anything to do with any kind of life. So poor, rats would visit but only stay a couple of days because we had so many hungry all kinds of snakes twisted up in our country style lifestyle. I hated snakes, but they loved us, judging by the way they scared the shit out of me every time I almost stepped on one of them. One day a snake fell out of a tree onto my shoulder. Grandmamma said I was lucky. I think she was lying. How can a green snake on your shoulder be a sign of luck? Anyway, as a whole, we were lucky to be living in Hampstead. Every Thanksgiving and every Christmas, the White people would bring to the front door of our shack a turkey with trimmings, oyster dressing, some make of cake. Sometimes they would leave at the door an apple pie, a cherry pie or a pecan pie. My favorite was pecan pie, but we never had any ice cream to flow across the top of apple pie or pecan pie. Every deer season either one of the three Jesuses would send a great White hunter to share, kindly, with us his kill. Venison pot roast, venison hamburgers, venison sliced thin and pan fried with wild onions, just as good as the nearest restaurant that didn't exist in my childhood Hampstead town. One time the Sheriff's brother-in-law, Billy Batts, bought us a mess of black bear meat. It must've been road kill, it smelled like it. They wouldn't eat it, they thought we would, but we didn't. We fed it to the crows. Between holidays, before and after, the fish houses and salt waters were plentiful of flounder and multitudes of unimaginable fish: Virginia mullet, popeyed mullet, spots, brim, grouper, sea shad, sea trout, red bass, black bass, croaker, rock fish. Fish houses, saltwaters and White people were good to us. They defined without proper articulation, the beauty of our country-life poverty poetry written, stanza by verse, upon the patience of trees and leaves that sometimes forgot to fall before early December.

Interestingly enough, in ways I can't quite put my finger on, even to this day, racism is different, kinder, almost humane when you live, as we did, "next door" to the one who defines himself, herself, as a racist. There is something idiosyncratic about being able to see through a wall that only avails itself to the seers if both sides are looking from and in the same nautical direction. A country mile is just as wide as it is long. I know because we walked everywhere we went. Joe Bill would always be going in a direction different from the way we were walking. Grandmamma always said he, too, was Heaven sent because he never grew tired of walking with the walking road gods of nice walking days, picking up beer cans and soda pop bottles.

Living in Hampstead, I knew who the Ku Klux Klansmen were, played baseball with their sons, knew how long a couple of their daughters' blond hair cascaded, sat watching Saturday morning cartoons in their living rooms, dined on fried chicken, potato salad and sweet tea at many of their kitchen tables. My first real job was working as a short-order cook for a Klansman. His name was, well I won't tell you his name, anyway, he was a solid citizen of a community located about fifteen miles south of Hampstead. He knew I knew, still he loved me because I was a good, hard working Colored country boy. Yes, he fired me from being a hamburger short-order cook because I burned too many hamburgers to justify my wages as a.... From then on, I was the ice cream dipping boy. They loved me, he loved me, and his sort of ugly daughters loved me too much for comfort in that tight space behind the ice cream counter. Almost every screaming kid that wanted a scoop, wanted chocolate like me.

My family, Grandmamma and five Black boys, and one other family were the only Colored people who were granted, given permission, I guess, to live in Whitetown (Hampstead) during my growing up years. Our mutual shacks were hollering distance close, connected by a dirt car-rut road, well-traveled, well-worn by deer hunting, coon hunting, White hunting-boy pickup trucks. The truck ruts were wide. They were especially appreciated because they allowed us to walk in the center of the rut and away from border grass rattlesnakes and ticks. Country-life loved us country boys because we respected the limitations as much as we respected the plentifulness of having just enough on a daily basis to make unintended racist ends meet their maker one by one, uniformly, as if planned by a power higher than any of us riding on that same country-life poverty bus, trying to figure out the shortest distance between two points on a race map, a map that mapped for us the ugly and the good, the misunderstanding of not being understood.

The other Colored family, Naomi Moore and Simon Jones, lived about a football field distance from us. I knew every step because in the years when our red pump handle would not prime water, I had to carry buckets of water from their scattered-red-hens-one-rooster yard to our backdoor steps. 100 yards, 500 steps, two sloshing buckets of freshly pumped water spilling small puddles all along the way. Naomi was half Iroquois and half something else. She was a ghost seer. And she never forgot to tell us, in vivid detail, the ghost stories of her encounters. Sometimes, while walking at night, she would tell me to step aside so I wouldn't step right into the face of a ghost. I always thanked her because the last thing I wanted to do was kiss a ghost in the mouth. Simon, I don't think they were married, was four quarters crazy and then some change. He couldn't read or write his name, and he only knew how to count one dollar bills, so all the White people he worked for paid Simon in one dollar bills. Simon was the simplest of simple men. Simple Simon didn't know how dumb he was and didn't care to know anything beyond the counting of one dollar bills. He counted plenty, doing simple jobs for White folks like mowing lawns and cemeteries, cleaning out hen houses, and taking trash to the trash pile. Simple Simon would always be sitting on top of the trash in the back of some White man's pickup truck, whistling as he kept the loose white trash from blowing away. Simon never brought home anything from the trash pile. He didn't think he needed any white trash, I guess.

If rumors are correct, the mythmakers have it that one summer the Topsail High School (my Hampstead, White, hometown high school which I was not allowed to attend until integration came like a storm) principal hired Simon to do some cleaning of classrooms and bathrooms. On this particular day, Simon was up on the 3rd floor, mop in hand, washing the math and science classroom floor, pre-counting one dollar bills when he heard a voice. The principal was down on the 1st floor doing what principals do in summer when teachers are not around. Anyway, the principal decided it was time to knock off for the day, as they say in farm-field terminology. So he called Simon over the intercom, "Simon, you ready?" Simple

Simon had never heard the voice of an intercom speak, had no earthly idea where the voice was coming from, thought it was the voice of God calling forth for him to come on "home." Confused beyond his normal state of delusion, Simon jumped out of the 3rd floor window. Hat in hand, he landed in a bed of boxwood bushes, not a scratch. "Simon, you ready?" running in his mind, but not as fast as Simon was running through the woods behind the school. Jesse Owens running in the 1936 Olympic Games couldn't have caught Simon that day.

Simon and Naomi, an odd couple to say the least, to say the most, but they loved us. They treated us as if we were the children God never intended for them to bring into that Hampstead White way of seeing that the world was indeed flat and divided. Christopher Columbus should've stayed in Spain, if you ask Simon. But nobody ever did ask Simple Simon anything about the divided flatness of anything but one dollar bills. Simon's family lived in Topsail, another railroad track, Black community just north of Hampstead. Everyone was afraid of Simon's mother because they said she worked "roots," a kind of Southern African American version of Voodoo. Most of Simon's family was sort of "sideways" in some kind of way. Naomi was what I would call a good kind of being weird. She was always giving us something to eat. Her refried collards and cornbread were the best I have ever eaten. Grandmamma tried to duplicate the menu, but "Naomi" was always the missing ingredient.

Grandmamma Ruth and Naomi were the best of best friends. Ruth and Naomi, they walked the roads and wooded paths of Hampstead, North Carolina as if they walked right out of the Old Testament, The Book of Ruth. And you could see it, feel it, hear it when they were together, going to blueberry fields to pick blueberries, going to flower fields to cut tulip flowers, going to tobacco farms to tie tobacco leaves onto tobacco sticks. Ruth and Naomi, they often went into the Hampstead woods to pull dog tongue, a wild tobacco-like crop that grew thick in rattlesnake country. They would lay out their batches, let their batches dry out on bed sheets spread out across the front yards of hot summertime suns. When all was cured and dry, they would hire a man with a truck to take their batches to market. Always, the money they made ended up in the cash register at Mr. Kye Howard's grocery store located in the center of Hampstead between the summer and winter smells of two fish houses and three Jesuses, too prim and too proper to smell like racism at all. I loved going to Mr. Kye Howard's store. I loved going back to the meat counter and talking to Straighty, the butcher, because he always made me and everybody else laugh with the un-cutting edges he spun around bad jokes. But what I most liked about going to the meat counter in Mr. Kye Howard's store and listening to Straighty was a chunk of sharp cheddar cheese chased with a bottle of Pepsi Cola. Those were wonderful days in ways that defy measurement when you measure with a Black and White measuring stick.

A summer morning photograph, all of us except Simon, on the side of the road, Highway 17, just down from being in front of the store, waiting for Aunt Lockey's blueberry bus to crest the hill and take us to blueberry fields where we would pick blueberries for a living during blueberry picking season. Before that it was strawberry picking season. After that was tobacco cropping time. In tobacco fields I met, face to face, the ugliest worm in the whole wide world, a green unicorn headed tobacco worm, full of green tobacco juice meanness. A frequent sight not wanted to be seen by anyone. Tobacco season was a three and a half parts season: priming season, cropping season, and putting-up season. Putting-up season was curing tobacco season. The men would put up sticks tied from end to end with green tobacco waiting to be cured. A few inside the barn and more outside, the men would line up and hand stick after stick until the first stick reached the sweating, brave soul at the top of the inside of the barn. There he would hang each stick on rafters, working his way across and down until the barn was full. Then the flames were lit. Grading the tobacco was kind of a half season and came about three weeks later. The "pennies" we made in tobacco fields and all other fields was rent free profit. The summer money I made was usually spent on school clothes and paper and pencils. For some reason, I've never tried to explain, I've always loved the yellow school bus color of nicely sharpened yellow pencils.

Living rent-free in our poverty designed each of us to believe that ends will always meet, designed each of us to know that God will always make a way. From our perspective, not believing in God was a privilege our poverty could not afford. Most days the only thing we had that was solid enough to hold onto was faith. Each Sunday morning we walked to church. Joe Bill would always be walking away from going to either one of the three White churches of Whitetown. Picking up bottles and cans was the closest he ever got to God, I suppose. Anyway, from right out of Whitetown into the always loving arms of Browntown, we walked. Two miles one way, winter, summer, I don't recall the walk ever being long and cold or long and hot. I just remember the sweating and shivering rhythms of faithful steps, one at a time. Yet, I am sure, at times, it was bitingly cold and unbearably hot, but Grandmamma was unrelentingly religious, and she believed, so we believed without question. We believed the weather forecaster would always be kind and considerate of and to us because we had nothing else to believe.

I remember the unembarrassed sheer pleasure of having no money to put into the St. John's church collection plate. I remember the sheer pleasure of sitting in church on hard bench seats listening to my cousin, Preston Lee's velvet, Negro gospel voice lifting the whole congregation up through the church house ceiling, on up to the pearly gates of a Negro Heaven. Then Preston Lee would let the congregation down softly, soulful as a Donny Hathaway and Roberto Flack duet, spinning the congregation like a long playing record on a soul saving turntable. Preston Lee Howard, that boy could sing like no tomorrow is tomorrow and the day after tomorrow if and if not it decides to come. Swaying, the whole congregation waving at the wind like leaves in breeze. "Precious Lord, take my hand..." If I close my eyes, I can hear him now, "Precious Lord, take my hand..." Preston Lee could sing a string off of a violin, then put it back, untouched. That boy could sing. Lord knows, that boy could sing.

Grandmamma taught us to listen to the sounds of music, taught us to hear the words of a prayer, taught us to love the meaning of everyday, ordinary love. Just in the way she carried herself, she taught us. Just in the way she would walk the roads of Hampstead, North Carolina, like walking on her own real estate property, she taught us. The White folks, most of them, called my grandmamma Miss Ruth, and I never saw Miss Ruth go into the back door of any White person's home. She worked for many of them, but I almost never witnessed her do much domestic work. It was almost as if she was not the "Help" at all. Mostly what I saw was socializing, watching soap operas and drinking afternoon Southern sweet ice tea while I was outside playing in the front with the White boys and White girls next door, left and right and in between the things and places I grew up playing between.

Yes, I grew up between, as they say, "a rock and a hard place" and some other place I am yet to name. We lived between two fish houses, both of which I worked into trying to understand what I have never been able to articulate, the nuanced nature of race relationships. The novelist, James Baldwin, said White people give to Black people to relieve their White guilt. Grandmamma would always leave those White households with a big brown paper sack full of something given. Miss Ruth had credit at both of Hampstead's stores. I can't remember and can't count all the times Grandmamma sent me to ask some White woman, always a White woman, if she would lend Miss Ruth two or three dollars. Always I came back with whatever Miss Ruth asked me to ask for. One thing I do remember and can count quite well is that I never went back to any of those White ladies' houses and said, "Here's the payback money you loaned to Miss Ruth last week." Maybe she did pay them back, maybe she didn't, I don't know, but I know this, the White people of Hampstead, North Carolina embraced and unembraced race in a manner both meaningful and mean as if there was no difference between the two fish houses and the three Jesuses. That, too, I imagine, was partly and "holy" designed for White people's psychological comfort. Natural as natural, the way I see it, given the history of Hampstead in the greater picture of things to come: I got kicked out of that same high school, math and science, 3rd floor window that Simon Jones jumped from, landing in boxwood bushes. Unlike Simon, I knew how to tell the time of day, so I landed not to run, but upon a Buddha bush blossoming lotus flowers.

My childhood, as I said, was a happy childhood. This, by any means, is not to suggest that five Black boys growing up in Whitetown experienced little racial discrimination. We did, plenty. I believe I was eleven years old when a drunk White man put another pistol to my head and said, "Nigger what ya doing over here digging in my trash? Ya better take yo black ass way from here 'fore I blow yo fucking nigger head off." I walked away thinking that anything I would've found at the trash pile wouldn't have been worth that. Next week my brother, Tyrone, and I went back to the trash pile, found what I didn't find a week prior. I never saw him again, and I never told Grandmamma the drunk–pistol part of the story. I guess like Joe Bill telling half stories, I only told Grandmamma the other part of the story.

My Hampstead history book tells of the days when the White boys I had played with all my life turned and decided it was socially and politically correct to throw rocks at me, harass me. They called me nigger-night-water-bucket boy because they liked the way the words flowed. When I was old enough to go to town (Wilmington) by myself, some nights I would come back on the late night Sea Shore Bus Line bus. I would disembark across the road from Mr. Kye Howard's store and the Phillip 66 gas and service station, both of which would be closed by then. The Lea boys (the same name as the fish house) and five or six other White boys would be hanging out on a weekend night doing what bored teenage boys do. When they saw me, they would pick up rocks and hurl them across the road at me. Interestingly enough not one of those White-country-boy rocks was brave enough to hit me between the eyes as that Black-city-boy rock had done years before. When I saw the rocks coming, I turned away and into the darkness towards home, I walked. They would all jump into one car and come looking for me. I would lay down in the ditch and watch them cruise by. With no visible signs of any real intentions of finding me, they always cruised on down the road. Those White country boys were cowards, not really looking for real valor. They needed only the impressions pressed upon the nature of their ugly love, fake dislikes for the likes of people like me. And their nigger-boy words were just that, words uttered from the same voices I went hunting with, played baseball with, played football with, but did not go to church with because of the un-divine design of segregation and its uncaring aftermath ways of confusing what's wrong with what's right about integration.

Maybe it was their Savior that saved those White boys who called me "Nigger" as if it were my name, if ever they were saved. But it was the patience of trees and leaves that never fell, my great teachers that saved me from being digested by the cruel languages of poverty. One of my earliest and greatest teachers was a White man who owned Hampstead's roadside souvenir, tackle and bait shop. He carried everything a fishing man and woman needed to catch a fish including crab traps and nets for catching shrimps. He sold Venus flytraps, pitcher plants and cypress knot lamp bases to travelers, but mostly he sold Moon Pie cakes, Honey Buns,

Coke Cola and Pepsi Cola to the locals. His name was McKinley Millis. He had two daughters, Shirley and Judy, and a wife that talked real loud. His house was directly behind the store, almost attached. Many times when I was in the store, I could hear Miss Marie in the kitchen cooking, squabbling with pots and pans, trying to get recipes to cooperate with the stove. Mr. McKinley was not a teacher in the classic sense, but he was a classic teacher in every other sense. He was "enlightenment" without ever meaning to be. He never knew Siddhartha followed me everywhere I went. He never knew, never came to realize that when he taught me how to catch Venus flytraps, he taught me one of my life's greatest lessons. During Venus flytrap catching season, many mornings he would take me with him into the swamp. I'm sure water moccasins saw us, but rarely did we see one of them. Turtles and frogs seemed not to be interested in hiding their faces. I was a boy, pregnant with swamp questions. Whenever I would ask him "Why this or why that?" he would hesitate, but just for a moment and say, "If you look at something long enough, you can figure it out." I looked at them long enough to figure out that a Venus flytrap can trap racial hatred and bigotry as easily as it traps the wings of a common black swamp fly for lunch. I honor that teacher, that

White man, that Venus flytrap souvenir, roadside shop owner who without ever knowing was my first poetry teacher. He taught me that you have to look before you can see. He taught me that you have to listen before you can hear. He taught me to how to feel the stubborn cadence of a dancing cypress tree that makes ever so slightly, the sound of poetry.

My second poetry teacher was my 7th grade teacher, Mr. Willie Edward McGee. Mr. McGee drove the pencil, dim-yellow colored school bus that bused me out of Whitetown to a Negro school (Annandale) about two miles north of Hampstead. Mr. McGee was black as Miles Dewey Davis blowing a trumpet in the dark and just as mean if you couldn't see and hear the nuances between the gaps in his teeth when he spoke of his love for playing baseball. He taught the poetry of swinging a bat, the poetry of fielding a hot line drive, the poetry of drifting into foul territory to catch a high flying foul ball hit hard and deep to the warning tracks of his love of playing left field. In those days, each teacher taught every subject outlined for the grade level. Mr. McGee taught everything "hard." The year I was in Mr. McGee's class, I was the only student that managed to make an A. My end of the school year report card recorded an A in English Literature and Bs in everything else. Mr. Willie E. McGee, his walk, his talk, his suit jacket, his sports coat, his Oxford white shirt, the tie of his Windsor tied necktie, his always shining wingtip shoes were poetry. Seamlessly, he combined the sound a homerun ball makes with the physics of listening to a transistor radio. AM, opening day, baseball poetry always found the right station. Mr. McGee loved baseball more than, as they say, Negroes love chicken and collard greens after church service.

And then there was the wonderfully beautiful Miss Ann Snyder, a White 8th grade teacher, teaching her first and what became her last year at a Black school, Annandale Elementary. Miss Snyder moved to Hampstead from Asheville, North Carolina, the other side of the world from my perspective during those days. Annandale Elementary School was an eight classroom school with no cafeteria. Out back, next to the ballfield-playground was a hut-sized canteen that mostly sold things that were cheap and sweet like stale Honey Buns made stale on purpose for growing Negro children. Miss Ann Snyder loved teaching and she loved me because I paid attention to the way white chalk marks on black blackboards revealed a world of poetic colors of which I had never seen. I loved Miss Ann Snyder the way a young boy loves a pretty woman in a red, pretty dress. Everyone admired Miss Ann Snyder because her gait was straight and her heart was braver than the "fires" she had to walk into, daily, that one school year. I loved her not because she awarded me a certificate for Highest Academics that year, but because I earned it and she recognized it. In her thoughtfully inquisitive ways, she was able to feel the "need" in the way we felt, down to the very core of our emotions and more. She, steadfast, taught her way through the walls of race colored rooms and bricks of White-people discrimination against her because she cared about and fought against what White society projected (on purpose) to happen to us. I honor Miss Ann Snyder and Mr. Willie McGee in a black and white photograph taken the last days of my last segregated school year. Miss Anne Elizabeth Snyder and Mr. Willie Edward McGee posing for a picture, one black as coal, one white as a sheet of notebook paper, both honest as poetry, not loud, but crystal.

When finally the United States Government granted me the "right" to attend my Hampstead, hometown, Whitetown High School,

Topsail High School, I ironed and pressed my best school clothes and went. I waited for the school bus a long time before I saw something yellow in the distance. As it came more fully into view, I couldn't believe they had sent a brand new school bus to pick up me. It stopped, the flag extended out, I stepped on, careful not to appear as nervous as I was. Down the aisle, every White face looked at me without looking at me. Towards the back I situated my books on the first empty seat. Lost in school bus chatter, I didn't comprehend anything said until I heard the word "vote." I was voted the ugliest boy on the school bus that day because I was the only Black person on the school bus that day. Even the bus driver, gladly, put her ballot in the ballot box. It was a heartbreaking moment, but my heart was hard to break. I kept my pride that day. I already knew that in order for me to be granted the "right" to go to school, someone had to have stolen, taken away from me the "right" to go to school. No, I was not sad. In fact, I was glad I had ironed and pressed my school clothes that morning. As ugly as I was voted to be, I knew the creases in my khakis were straight. I knew I looked good for the first day of integrated school. As the teachings of Maya Angelo tells us, a caged bird can never forget how to fly.

I flew in, I walked into Honors English the first day of class and she was sitting there behind her desk wearing librarian, cat-eye eyeglasses propped up on the bullet-points of a not-too-tight sweater. Her eyes were the color of Ireland, Irish green, and she looked, in my mind, just like her name, Miss Mary Ellen Hart. She wasn't beautiful, she didn't wear beautiful dresses. Mostly she wore dull colored floral print patterns. Her shoes were old lady shoes, not poetic at all. But Miss Mary Ellen Hart's words were the words of Elizabeth Barrett Browning, the words of Edna St. Vincent Millay, the words of Christina Rossetti. Some days the good gray father himself, Walt Whitman, would come calling. Other days Langston Hughes and Claude McKay escorted the Harlem Renaissance into Miss Hart's classroom. The Harlem photographer, James Van Der Zee, came one day to take a portrait of me wearing Miss Hart's cat-eye eyeglasses. All the White students laughed at me, the ugliest boy in the classroom modeling school-teacher eye glasses. I knew I looked good, how could I have not, I looked just like my daddy. Plenty White women in Hampstead would always ask about my daddy when other White people were not within hearing distance. My White classmates laughed, but I was not a clown. I wanted to see the beautiful world of words the way Miss Hart saw the beautiful world of poetry. It was there in that laughing room that I fell in love one year before I got kicked out of the Pender County School System for inciting a riot I did not invent. Yes, right there in Miss Hart's classroom, listening to her sweet-unsweet voice, I fell in love with my first love, the writing of words. Two days less than one year later found me diagramming the composition of my last Topsail High School English class sentence, "He hit me first."

It was a warm for the season, early March day. The last period class had given way to basketball practice for the ones of us on the Topsail Pirates basketball team. The Topsail Pirates baseball team was having its first pre-spring training meeting. The baseball players (all White except for Roosevelt and Billy who were practicing with us because they were also on the basketball team) were situated at the other end of the gym, mostly watching us basketball players run half court drills, practice lay-ups and free throws. The coach, Mr. Carter, called for a set-motion play. For some reason Coach threw the ball to me. Facing the basket, I faked right and drove left, leaving the defense frozen in place. My shot had taken aim but had not left my left hand when I felt it. The tallest player on the team, a White boy whom I will not name, had drilled me with a deliberate elbow to the back of my head. I responded like I was Cassius Clay turning into Muhammad Ali, right jab, left uppercut, lights out, TKO. I don't know what happened next, all I know is the Black boys in the gym that day started body slamming the White basketball and baseball players like they were crash test dummies. In the foreground and the background, unpacked black and white packages addressed to color-code addressees. Mailroom Maelstrom Arena presented in black and white, three channel, technicolor television. The first scene without credits rolled over into the second scene with credits, spilling backlogs of anger onto and in between the aisles and hallways of every classroom. Pent-up frustrations released like explosive packages that had been waiting forever to be delivered. I was the postman, I suppose. I only did what postal workers do, put mail in mailboxes. Yet, my duty was found guilty of an unforgivable crime, a Black boy, an Honor Student with the highest standing in the class, standing up to blatant racism at Topsail High School, Hampstead, North Carolina in 1969. The same year Neil Armstrong walked on the moon, I walked the roads of my hometown-Whitetown for the very last time. The ugliest boy on the school bus was kicked out of the Pender County School System forever for inciting a riot he did not invent.

Displaced forever and nights without the calming salt water sounds of sound water to comfort me, I struck out, went down swinging. Strike three. I was sixteen, standing on the side of the road, Highway 17, the King's Highway. One hand in the pocket of a worn-out blue jean jacket, the other hand thumbing, trying to hitch a ride out from in between two fish houses and three Jesuses. I had no idea which direction Joe Bill was walking that day. I had no idea it would take me twenty-five and a half years to get to where I was going. From where I was standing, I couldn't quite see if any of the five White fish house-Jesuses was watching me. Out of view, still I felt the burning eyes of a White public school system that never did learn to love or appreciate the flow of my Colored, saltwater boy ways. Siddhartha was standing there beside me, paying attention to everything by not paying attention to anything, just as he always does. Silence never moves with notice, the patience of trees. Everything seemed stopped as if time does stand still sometimes.

And in my stillness of being still, I wondered if it was by divine design that I remembered that I loved Elvis Presley and Rick Nelson just like every White boy I knew. I loved Country and Western music just like every White boy I knew. My first girlfriend was White, my second girlfriend was White, my third girlfriend was White. Why? Was there a White core in me White enough to be loved? They all loved me, but never did I love a one of them. Ku Klux Klansmen's sheets were too Clorox white back then. My adoptive godmother, Miss Cora Mae Ward, was White. Miss Cora Mae claimed me as her Colored child to make her contest bid more competitive at the Methodist Church annual fundraising event. Her youngest daughter, Christine, my sister by default, was White. My best friend, Bobby Joe, was White. Though we didn't have a mailbox and rarely got any General Delivery mail, my mailing address was as White as any White mailing address in Hampstead, North Carolina, 28443. As you can or may not be able to imagine, some days my point of view was White as the snow Hampstead, North Carolina almost never got. REBECCA HOWARD was White. REBECCA, the name on a grave stone I walked past many times. She would always speak and tell me something nice, what,

I don't quite remember. All I remember is how much I loved Rebecca's voice. All the cemeteries in Hampstead were White. All the churches were White. The trash piles were White piles of White people's White lives. The broken-in-just-enough-places-to-be-fixed Real American Hero toy soldier I found at the trash pile was White. Every one of my baseballs was beaten-up White, but my baseball glove was always the color of me.

After not so long at all, a fast car stopped a bit beyond me, but what seemed like a fourth of a quarter mile from where I was standing. I quickly trotted up to catch up with a red Chevrolet Corvette with no back seat. Two drunk White marines still wearing their uniforms, escaping for the weekend, escaping from Camp Lejeune Marine Base (less than 35 miles north of Hampstead, North Carolina) were like mannequins, just sitting there. Both sets of soldier boy eyes damn near glued straight ahead like they were dead drunk. The passenger side mannequin marine figured his way out of his shotgun seat without giving me "the time of day," so I could fit myself in. My midnight dark frame contorted to fit so evenly along a beautifully elongated Corvette Sting Ray car console. Five speed shape-shifting stick between my dangling tennis shoes, strings untied. In that tight space behind the driver's seat, I squeezed a duffel bag full of everything I was trying to forget how to own. My afro slanted beautifully into the middle corner of a slightly tinted rear window view. My eyes facing up, looking up into a Carolina blue sky with not even a white hint of clouds to cloud and confuse my vantage point. I smelled only the smell of salt. Those two drunk White boy marines saved me that day. Nobody said a word until that red Corvette Stingray's speedometer said 95, 96, 97, 98, 99, 100 miles per hour wasn't fast enough.

Twenty-six years, five months and seventeen days later, finally I squeezed my way out of the fast pace tightness of a closed-in space. I felt like I was getting out of a spaceship, fresh back from circling the Negro side of the moon. I finally came down and touched the ground in San Francisco. I disembarked the California Zephyr, a passenger train operated by Amtrak between Chicago and the San Francisco Bay Area. Everything looked so familiar. It was clear, it was cool, almost cold and the Golden Gate Bridge looked as if she had been smiling at motorists and tourists the best and the better part of the morning.

Almost a month earlier, out of Chattanooga, I hitched a ride to Atlanta, bought a one-way 4-city-stop-get-back-on Amtrak train ticket to San Francisco. My stops included Philadelphia, six days; Chicago, a little over a week; Denver, three and a half days and Salt Lake City, five days and a night. She said her name was Anne. It was surreal from the beginning. I had just gotten off the train and I was looking for a bench seat as far away from the station as possible to rest my thoughts. She was already there, and she looked like she needed me to speak, so I said hello. For the next fifteen minutes she was like a can of beans that had been waiting for a can opener. She spilled out her life to me. She told me she was raised and grew up in Wilmington, North Carolina. She told me that she left her job working at Belk in the mall. She told me that she just walked out of her third marriage and she was not looking for a fourth. She told me she didn't have any children. She told me she graduated from John T. Hoggard High School, the Class of 1972 (the same school and year as me). She told me she was never going back for another class reunion. She told me Salt Lake City was not where she wanted to be. She told me a lot more stuff, I told her nothing. By the time I got ready tell her about me, a man wearing a dark suit appeared and off they went. I don't know what her real story really was, all I know is you can't get lost in Salt Lake City because from every vantage point you can still see the steeples of the Mormon Salt Lake Temple. Anne and Anne's story played out in black and white on a night of no moon. In me, she watched an ending unfold, in her, I smelled an opening, softly, slowly grow wider. Darkness reveals "light," surreal reveals "real."

It had been a long ride in a backseat that wasn't a backseat after all. Twenty-six and a half years I believed in every minute, most by mistakes that turned out not to be mistakes at all. I guess when Siddhartha follows you everywhere you go and you remember what your teachers told you years ago, listening to the patience of trees will guide you to good places you've never been to before. Then all of a sudden you realize that you are somewhere you intended to go twenty-six and a half years ago. You recognize the patterns of streets and signs, the flow of traffic. Your shoes know, within and without reason, where to step and where not to step. You look down as much as you look up because you grew up walking among rattlesnakes in your country life and card sharks in your city life. Crowds of people rushing to wherever crowds of rushing people go look like people you've seen before rushing up and down the streets of San Francisco. Amidst the hustle and bustle of sidewalks and crosswalks, you take your time, slow, like you remember walking through pine tree woods. Everybody knows your name, yet nobody does. You look both ways before crossing streets at safe-to-cross-now lights. You don't jaywalk because you are a country boy.

I started out at sixteen, standing on the grassy edge of the last highway on the East Coast, trying to hitch a ride as far away as I could get, the West Coast. Catching a fast car ride as far as the next town, I ended up in Wilmington, North Carolina. I guess that's as far as the road leading to California was willing to go and take me with it at that time. I unpacked my life, but I was never able to settle in, too much city noise for my *Saltlife* ways. For almost three years, living in Jervay Housing Projects, I endured the race of rats racing roaches to see which would not die first on the floors of housing project kitchens. I endured death at the door, the invite of heroin. Never did I look into the face of an off-white powdered syringe. I endured the sad lavishes of good-time Saturday night parties until someone would pull out a gun, and like each of our personal teams of cockroaches, we scattered. I endured the night my running partner, Rusty, was shot dead up at the Sea Horse Cafe. I was supposed to go with him that night. I have never been glad I didn't go with him. Maybe I could have saved Rusty that night. That's what running partners are made for when you live in housing projects. Rusty and his brother, Winslow, lived next door. His older sister Sweetie, I tried to love, but she never tried to love me. I endured school days when I didn't learn a thing. The teachers were too preoccupied with designing order out of chaos. Excited, incited as riot books of no knowledge. For meaning, I read between lines. I endured the smoke of race-war-seasoned crossfires burning down my town one block at a time. A gambler's life, I lived. Inner city, red brick, project life is a chance-taking life. You bluff without a life to pay, you bluff and pray no one calls your bluff.

Drafted into the military before I finished high school, Uncle Sam let me graduate before sending me to Lackland Air Force Base, San Antonio, Texas for basic training. Man, that Texas sky is big, still it wasn't as blue as Carolina blue. After basic training, I was sent to Sheppard Air Force Base in Wichita Falls, Texas for technical school training. My first duty assignment stationed me at Pope Air

Force Base, located in the middle of Fort Bragg Army Base, Fayetteville, North Carolina, just ninety miles from Wilmington. Every weekend I would hitchhike home. Everyone thought I was crazy because I loved thumbing rides so much. But you know what, there's nothing like it. Your first ride dropped you off where one country road intersects with another country road. In the middle of nowhere the two roads cross out everyday static. You walk to a place where you are, you're standing on the grassy edge of a two lane highway, not a car in sight either direction. Cows and horses in fields pay you no attention as if even you standing there in plain sight are invisible. You don't know if a car will ever come, you don't know if you will ever make it to wherever you're headed. You don't know anything, but you feel everything. Out there on the road, for a while you are the only human being in the whole wide world. Zen. It's a beautiful feeling to be that alive.

I have always loved suitcases, and my suitcase was open and ready to be packed for a trip somewhere, anywhere when my orders arrived telling me to report to Clark Air Force Base, Philippines, no later than September 19th, 1974. I married my high school sweetheart, Faye, just before I was shipped out to the Philippines. After a year of monsoon rain and trying to but not avoiding the chew of sugar cane, my wife joined me. Our daughter, Rashida, was conceived in the tall mountains of that volcano island. Eleven years of a way-up and way-down marriage stopped at a red light one night, then forgot to notice when lights change to green, you go. It had been my fault from the beginning. I have always been a bad liar, I've always tried to tell the truth. The light looked green, but truth is it stayed red too long. From then on we drove separate cars down separate streets only to end up in the same place, unmarried to each other, yet still in love.

As a kid I don't recall ever wanting to go to college. I just wanted to be wise and wander the roads of America like Jack Kerouac long before I knew Jack Kerouac lived most of his life on the road. So yes, I never intended to go to college, but after 4 years and 9 months in the Air Force, that mistake granted me the GI Bill. Afraid that the GI Bill would run out before I finished and because I needed to make up for lost time, having stayed back in the 3rd grade because I was dyslexic and recited my ABCs backwards (not really, but close) better than I recited them forward, I completed the requirements for a BA in Social Science and

Philosophy in record time, three years. I didn't take off summers, I went to every summer session for three years straight. Three years straight, Dr. Denis didn't say a thing when we smoked pot in class every time he decided to have class outside. Dr. Denis called himself a Jewish boy from Brooklyn, and he talked just like a Jewish boy from Brooklyn. For three years I took every Philosophy class he taught. We students followed him around campus like he was Socrates. He told us that the definition of aesthetics was to be on a sinking ship, in the middle of the night, in the middle of the ocean, in the middle of a thunderstorm and be able to see the beauty of flashes of lightning against the pitch-black backdrop. Almost every class he would tell us some version of, "If I say it's raining outside, don't take my word for it, go to the window and look for yourself."

Diploma in hand, my first professional job, if you want to call it that, was selling used cars. I learned a valuable lesson selling used cars. "If you can sell a used car, you can sell anybody anything anytime." So I sold anybody any piece of junk for a little over a year, and won the Salesman of the Year Award. My selling lemons award led to a successful job interview at the Cape Fear Crisis Hotline Center. I guess they thought that if I could talk people into buying a-piece-of-shit car, I could talk people out of putting guns to their heads. I answered hotline calls, 48 hours on, 48 hours off for 18 months, then I got promoted to director of one of the agency's other program components, TASC (Treatment Alternatives to Street Crime). I was a street crime, myself, by most definitions, but I wasn't on drugs and I didn't need any treatment, so I fit the bill, I guess. After three years and just when I was in line and had a good chance at being named State Director of TASC programs for the State of North Carolina, I gave my two-week notice two weeks early.

To this day I don't know who or what told me I should go to graduate school and get an MFA in writing. Maybe it was my dead father. Daddy died when I was nineteen, two months before I was inducted into the Armed Services, or maybe it was my dead Grandmamma Ruth, she waited until I came back from the Philippines to die. Anyway, after I graduated with a BA in Philosophy and Social Science from the University of North Carolina at Wilmington, I regularly hung out with my former poetry professors and poetry students. Maybe that was it, I don't know. I believed in logic about as much as logic believed in me. So, most likely, it was some unspoken vibe I finally paid full attention to when I decided to listen. Siddhartha followed me everywhere I went. The poetry professors and their students published citywide literary magazines, but they never would consider my poetry good enough to claim a place in one of their "prestigious" journals. Still I went to a lot of poetry readings, drank a lot of red wine, ate a lot of cheese, and in the late Eighties, together we built the literary center of downtown Wilmington. Just before I left town, Dino De Laurentiis brought a Hollywood cast to our town and made a crazy movie, *Blue Velvet*, which I love. The poetry professors, their poetry students and I used to attend Black Velvet whiskey tasting parties in the Cape Fear Hotel where parts of *Blue Velvet* were filmed.

So in the waning years of that Eighties-music decade, I purchased my first brand new, right-off-of-the-top-shelf suitcase and hitched a ride to the airport. Two years later, the Vermont College of Norwich University bitter cold winter weather awarded me an MFA in Writing degree with emphasis in poetry. My degree landed me a job teaching creative writing and African American Literature at the University of Tennessee at Chattanooga. Leaving Chattanooga after my job interview, boarding pass in hand, getting ready to board a 1-stop-over flight to Charlotte, North Carolina, I looked back. Right there on an empty chair was an unfolded *USA Today* full page announcement for the movie, *Dead Poets Society*. Always looking for something to read on the plane, I would have gotten it, but the ticket agent lady was already reaching for my boarding pass. We landed in Charlotte, I unbuckled my seat belt, eased down the aisle and into a waiting gate, waiting for arrivals. To the left, just as it was in the Chattanooga Airport, laying upon an empty chair right there in the Charlotte Airport, the same unfolded *USA Today* full page announcement for the movie, *Dead Poets Society*. I claimed that copy as my copy. I believed it much more than I couldn't believe it. At that very quiet moment when everything stopped, Zen and there I knew my Wilmington, North Carolina bound airplane flight would land me a university tenure-track teaching job at the University of Tennessee at Chattanooga.

Without an English degree, working in the English Dept. was never a challenge for me. I remembered everything my teachers told me, and I told my students everything they had said. I remembered how much my teachers loved me, so I poured love, unfiltered, upon my students. I remembered my childhood shack where the grass refused to grow, so I planted fertile seeds in the fertile black soils of students hungry to grow. Beyond the season, the grass grew green. Within the first five years, I won two SGA Professor of the Year Awards and the University of Tennessee National Alumni Association Outstanding Teacher Award. Not bad for a country boy without a higher education plan. Pretty good for a country boy elected into the Topsail High School Freshman Class of 1968 as "The Ugliest Boy on the School Bus." Accomplishments in the dark often go unnoticed. Siddhartha must have noticed, but Siddhartha's face is blank, never a smile, never a frown. The patience of trees is a virtue. Without knowing I was waiting, I had waited.

In 1995 I was awarded a Summer Fellowship. My project proposal was to travel across the country and write a novel, working title *Looking for Jack Kerouac*. With a copy of *On the Road* tucked in my cargo pants pocket, I packed a 3 ft. tall Alpine climbing Mt. Everest backpack, left the stove on, hoping the house would burn down (just kidding) and went out the door. I was on the road again just like Willie Nelson, pot pipe in my other cargo pants pocket. I left singing a Motown music song. I looked in Kerouac's haunts, high and low, as I walked across cities and towns all along the way. In my paisley book, I wrote what I saw, what I smelled, what I heard in languages only school bus yellow pencil marks could read. I measured the amount each paisley book page would hold, mostly, between train stops and the patience of remembered young trees. I looked around corners, down alleyways and in between places somebody forgot how to name. I talked my way into the lives of train riding people and people who could not remember where they used to live. Some smelled like, acted like they had been beaten years ago by the Beat Generation. Some even looked a lot like Jack Kerouac, but I never did find a Jack Kerouac that looked exactly like the Jack Kerouac photograph on the back cover of *On the Road*. What I found was the picture-painted voice behind Kerouac's words. Finally I could see what I heard when I heard the rains of Kerouac's Denver pages of *On the Road*, "At lilac evening I walked...in the Denver Colored section, wishing I were a Negro, feeling that the best the White world had offered was not enough ecstasy for me, not enough life, joy, kicks, darkness, music, not enough night..."

Yes, the blue voice of that quote put together for me a picture of what I was really looking for when I set out to find the meaning of why Kerouac spent his "life" on the road. Kerouac was looking for the meaning of what it means to be born dark like me. All my life I had been a man in motion, seeking to find what was at the heart and soul of the way so many White people treat so many Black people. What is racism made of? I have thought, "What if?" "What if you were in a biology lab and you dissected a racist attitude?" What answers would the parts reveal? I have been discriminated against, called nigger, spat at, told to go back to Africa so many times, I simply wanted to search out the mechanical makeup of what I call the White noise machine. Only machines that are oiled well can hurl effortlessly. According to Kerouac, White America loves and needs the dancing dark jazz movements of her Black people. In the language of Ugly Love, "White guilt as defined as a repercussion of slavery" is clearly delineated, line by line, on both sides of every page in every dictionary in every city, every small town, everywhere across this land, America the Beautiful—America the Ugly.

So in biology lab dissection class, your first semester, take a scalpel and cut into the word "racism" and you will find that the part labeled *envy* is what holds together all the other emotional components of a racist attitude. Why *envy*? Because Black people are born, live and die embodying the improvisational nature of jazz. "Everybody wants that," Kerouac said. Kerouac loved jazz. Kerouac's Buddha was Bird (Charlie Parker). Bird's saxophone carried Kerouac from New York City to Mexico City. Kerouac wrote novels like musical compositions. Jack Kerouac wrote blues poetry the same way Bird played jazz saxophone. Both sweating the music of words and notes until they were drunk as never been drunk like this, celebrating the improvisation of Negro improvisation.

Take a look at this: No matter how poor, impoverished, Black people find themselves, they are not mean and sad because of their conditions. They may be down, but they are seldom out. They dance and sing and smile and have a good time with whatever they have as if they have whatever it is they don't have. One of William Faulkner's White characters said to another White character, "If you could be a nigger on a Saturday night, you would never want to be a white man again." What is William Faulkner trying to tell us? Is he talking about the improvisational nature of jazz? Kerouac said so and I know so.

I know the wrong answer is not always wrong, and the right answer is not always right. I know every angle that expresses itself as this or that has to be measured for the accuracy of this or that. I remember when I was a kid growing up in Whitetown, the 90 feet from home plate to 1st base did not equal the 90 feet from 3rd base to home plate. Why, because the latter is longer and puts a score on the scoreboard. I ran so fast, I didn't know that then. Now, I am slow. The answer is always the answer, this I have always known. How could I have not? Growing up Black in a Whitetown, I saw gleamingly dull examples every day in the way White people would smile at us without smiling at Black people in general, be kind to us and somewhat considerate of us and not pay any special attention to Black people in general. Perhaps all that was needed was a scalpel to cut into the value of a smile. What quantitative value does White America assign (along race lines) to what's valid and what's not worth the time of a White world day? I am sure Siddhartha knew all along what I needed, but he has never told me anything. It's just that I learned to "look" by looking at the way he never looks at me. The answer is always in the question and hard questions are always written in Latin. So, it was understanding how as a kid I understood by looking, looking at something long enough to figure out the measurements of balance needed to walk train track rails without falling off, looking at something until it showed me the way to interpret Latin phases in three flourishing opera movements of understanding.

My first night on the train out of Atlanta came to be my first night of understanding (1st movement). That night I meet Spencer in the viewing car. Spencer, a 20-year-old White boy from the wealthy center of Meridian, Mississippi. Rich as Richie Rich, but he was not a funny papers cartoon character. He was uniquely rich. According to Spencer, he had been kicked out of his family for bad behavior. Leaning back in his seat, legs crossed like the aristocratic prep school boy he was, he invited me to sit at a conversational angle from where he was sitting. He was going to Philly to find another handle to hold onto, I imagined. The only luggage he carried was a set of the most expensive golf clubs ever made, alluded to as he told me how light he was traveling. He had a pocket full of airplane bourbon bottles, he offered me more than a few. On into the night we talked about his getting kicked out of Mississippi State and Ole Miss. I never asked why, he never told me why, so we let the night hitch a ride to Philly on those two facts unexplained. He was chain smoking Marlboro Reds. Between drags and puffs and sips, he asked, "Now Hudson (my name in the novel and the name I introduced myself to him as) what are you writing in that paisley book?" Before I could answer, years went by before he said, "I know what you're writing in that book, I know everything." "Everything?" More years went by as I thought back to what my Venus flytrap teacher said when I would ask him a question, "If you look at something long enough, you can figure it out." Somewhere on one of his golf courses, on the front nine or the back nine, Spencer had learned the lessons of "Just Looking." Though I was writing a novel, Spencer looked at the night angle of my dark face and saw that I was nobody but a lost poet, trying to write my way out from being in between. I had no further questions. Siddhartha was on the train and Spencer and I were drunk, getting drunker as miles of countryside flew by. Amtrak train speed canceling towns and cities on a train line map, crossing state lines and other borders that had no way of knowing they were borders between races of people. The Russian poet Yevgeny Yevtushenko said, "First we form the borders, and then the borders form us." Back in my train seat later that night, I thought about how the borders of Whitetown had forced me to fall in love with the movement of suitcases. Some train rides are always smooth. "Everything," he had said, "I know everything."

My second night of understanding (2nd Movement) was a night in Chicago, the night I met Allyson. Allyson was beautiful in the classic sense you see when you watch a classic movie. Her bouncing red Rita Hayworth red hair cascaded almost stealing from her face. Her legs were the legs of a television commercial whether you watch primetime or not. Allyson was wearing a red lipstick look that would make runway models look twice before crossing the runway. Her skin was milk white like Black Irish white. Each of her fingers wore a different color of nail polish and each without a ring except both thumbs. I was in my second year of growing dreadlocks and they loosely locked against my shoulders. Allyson and I locked eyes as we were claiming our luggage from our in-bound train. We spent the night up into the wee hours trying to find the combination to the combination lock that locked our eyes. We never could. As she grabbed her duffle bag which had been leaning against my Jack Kerouac backpack I said, "You were on my train." "What makes it your train, maybe it's mine," Allyson said. At that moment I fell in love with Allyson's voice just as she was falling in love with mine. After we stowed away our luggage in the train station lockers, we walked the best and the better part of the night away. Up and down the Magnificent Mile (North Michigan Ave.), crossing Clark Street and LaSalle Blvd., Dearborn Street, Orleans Street and Lake Shore Dr. On State Street we stopped for almost an hour, listening to a jazz saxophone man play mostly Bird and Charlie Mingus music. We walked up mean streets, down un-mean streets, up broad-way streets, across alleyways, under El train bridges, stopping for coffee here and a sandwich there. We found every light in Chicago that night, every one of them in the reflection of one store front window after another. When our locked eyes could handle no more light and our voices were weak for sleep, we fell asleep in an abandoned corner of the Amtrak station waiting room. "Was that a dream?" woke me up. Allyson was nowhere to be seen, not a sign. A train station clock that said 8 o'clock in all 24 time zones told me how confused I was, and I had to pee like no morning had ever told me to go pee. In the train station restroom, an attendant handed me a paper towel as I walked up to the sink. Before I turned on the water, I looked into a train station restroom mirror. There firmly planted upon my forehead, a red lipstick kiss. I don't know how long I stood looking, don't know if I ever did wash my hands, don't know what the paper towel man thought. All I know is what I remember saying to that train station mirror, "Jack Kerouac will be a lot easier to find after Allyson." I stumbled into the morning thinking out loud, "Mr. Bartender, please, I need a drink, a double shot of anything, nothing but rocks."

Someone once said to me, "There are no conclusions to be made, all conclusions have already been made." I don't know if I believe that or not, but, so as I said, after a twenty-six year trip, I arrived in San Francisco with a head full of frost. Everyone was wearing a jacket (3rd movement). It was the middle of June. I was looking for Jack Kerouac in Jack Kerouac Alley next to City Lights Bookstore on Columbus Ave. when I stumbled upon my third understanding. When I first arrived in San Francisco, I rented a by-the-week motel room in the Mission District, about a 30 minute always-crowded-bus-ride from where I met a street man named Fromm. Fromm looked like why the Germans tried to claim Aryan superiority. He was tall, blond, blatantly handsome with pool water blue, cool weather blue eyes that pierced when pointed in any wind direction. The creases in the Army fatigue jacket he was wearing were starched at full military attention. The afternoon I stopped and told him I was in town looking for Jack Kerouac, he offered me a hit from the roach of a pencil thin he was smoking and said, "Can't help you there, soldier." How did he know I had served? I wondered as I thought about Spencer. Fromm made his living asking for money, not begging for money. Fromm was a street man without looking like a street man. His clean clothes fit perfectly his clean cut demeanor. With his James Dean looking face and James Dean acting attitude, he preyed on tourist ladies in comfortable walking shoes and busy business women walking the streets of San Francisco in high heels and gay boys revealing preference by gait. "Standing right here, I make a hundred dollars on a bad day," he said. When I showed him a copy of my poetry book, *Hat Dancer Blue*, he just looked at the cover for a long time then said, "There's this place you should check out, a bookstore, they might let you read, tell them you know me." Then he took out a pencil and proceeded to draw a map inside of the cover of my book. Asked me if I wanted another hit, handed the book back to me and said, "This is how you get there, you might find

Jack whatever you said his name was hanging out down there." We fist-bumped and I was off. "Take care, Hudson," he not quite yelled above the noise of car and street cars on the streets of San Francisco in the cool of that Bay Area afternoon.

After learning a lesson of not buying two California burritos for a mid-afternoon lunch, I made it to the bookstore that Fromm had drawn on a map. I stood outside before going in, taking tiny hits from the pencil thin joint Fromm had nonchalantly slipped to me during our fist-bump-see-ya. Some bookstores are more literary than others, this was the top of the line. I don't think they could get any more books in there. The bookstore owner was a man without direction, scattered like loose pages and wind. Yet, he seemed to pay attention and not pay attention at the same time. So when he told me he had two poets scheduled to come in from London for a next Friday night reading, and that he would put me on the Friday night bill, I had to believe my ears and not believe my ears all at the same time. He didn't talk out of both sides of his mouth, he talked twice out of the same side. At least that's the way I thought I heard his words after hitting that pencil thin again.

Come Friday, sure enough my name was on the Friday Nite 7 p.m. playbill. My name, Hudson Rivers, the third name in red chalk marks on a sign out in front of the bookstore. It was close to 6:30 when I walked in, *Hat Dancer Blue* in my satchel, ready to be read. No one, not a sound in the room. I checked again, no one, not a sound in the room. I'm not sure what I was feeling at that moment, but apparently that moment was feeling me. On the checkout counter there was a copy of *Poets and Writers* opened to a page. In the lower right hand corner of that page there was a contest announcement: Jack Kerouac International Literary Prize. I couldn't believe my eyes, yet I must have believed my eyes. August of the next year, I won the 7th Annual Jack Kerouac International Literary Prize. "After Allyson" the Chicago chapter of *Looking for Jack Kerouac* must have locked the judge's eyes, and like me, he or she could not find the right combination of numbers to unlock Allyson's lipstick look combination lock.

After the reading, I took the bus back to my Mission District rent-by-the-week room. There, sitting in a paisley chair reading pages I had written in my paisley book, the dim motel room lamp reminded me of the dim kerosene lamp light that read translated Pushkin fairy tales to me when I was a kid, wild as weeds. I thought about drifting back and forth across center field, robbing White boys of home runs. I thought about stealing 2nd base, thought about stealing home plate the way Jackie Robinson used to do. I thought about the science of digging through a White-people trash pile, looking for white trash and finding my Jim Bowie knife.

I thought about my brother Lee's face beneath a pale Hampstead moon. Later that evening, we were supposed to go night fishing. I thought about my grandmamma watching me clean fish and watching all three of us, at the same time, riding that one bicycle we got for Christmas that one year. I remember her praying that none of us would fall. I thought about our little shack house and the front yard grass that refused to grow for Colored people. I thought about George Washington's eyes looking down upon me from the top of a live oak tree. I thought about Gypsy Rose Lee and her beautifully rich, but poor kids in the back seat of a snapbean green Gypsy-mobile. I thought about my mother, Idell Nixon Braggs, the Queen of Browntown, on a bus going and coming back from New York City. My mother loved suitcases as much I do. I thought about the chapter in Mom and Dad's story that they decided not to read to me. I thought about baby boy Lee and how both my brother Lees were named after Daddy's best friend, Lee Scott. I thought about my father's white teeth, gleaming, when I told him I was going into the Air Force. I remember what he said to me two months before he died, "Now you can fly, son."

Yes, there in that paisley colored arm chair, I thought about my baby sister, Monica, born just before I left home for the Armed Forces. Monica, born of a father that was not our father, yet loved by each of us as if it were beyond the case. Monica didn't know who I was when I came home from the Philippines. I thought about how in post-riot years, she got a job working at that same (crossfire) KFC as soon as she turned working age. I thought about rooms of smoke in Mrs. Davis' 11th grade English Literature classroom. At John T. Hoggard High School, Mrs. Davis was the only teacher I loved. When my first book of poetry, *Hat Dancer Blue*, was published in 1992, Mrs. Irene Davis was the first, the very first, to send a letter of congratulations to me. It had been twenty-one years since I was in her class. Surprised, I was not, yet I was surprised by my tears. I guess I needed Mrs. Davis to smile upon me again. I thought about my other teachers that I still loved, Mr. McGee, Miss Anne Snyder and Mrs. Hart, and how they each took turns drawing direction for me to follow. I thought about Venus flytraps. I thought about the fish house and the school house that expelled me for life because I wouldn't sit down, be still and be quiet as told to do so. I thought about the three Jesuses that unintentionally helped raise me and how each was afraid to disagree with the politics of segregation. Any one of them could've taken down that "sign," but none dared try. I thought about how each white church steeple in my childhood Hampstead, North Carolina was broken off at the top.

I thought about that lady from Omaha, Nebraska, and the secret she told me. I thought about Negro gospel choirs singing the spirituals of jazz deep into the heart of an early Sunday afternoon, thought about my cousin, Preston Lee. "Lord knows that boy can sing," the Browntown church ladies used to say. I don't think I will ever get his velvet singing voice out of my head, and I don't want to. I thought about Alphonso and Alonzo, the twins, they grew up singing in the church choir. I thought about my great-grandmother, Hattie Brown Nixon, who lived next door to St. John's Church, who lived to be almost a 100 years old. I thought about the fish fry after her funeral, thought about the picture of me she kept on the fireplace mantel. I thought about what President John F. Kennedy meant to Colored people back then when I was a kid sitting in the sun on the back porch of a shack.

Yes, there in that paisley colored chair, sitting beneath the light of a dim lamp light, I thought about the contrast of black and white, the contrast of city life and country life. I remembered each, and how each was a kind of living in a "black box life." I thought about sinks full of roaches and riots and our war clothes drying in the weariness of riot-torn sunshine. The front line was the clothesline in my backyard. The smell of teargas, I don't think ever dies. I thought about Willie Earl, thought about the sticks of his drum set beating out beautiful riffs but not beating beautifully enough to beat the Wilmington Ten charges levied against him. I thought about my own brother, Tyrone, up on Castle Street one riot-torn night holding the police at bay from atop a three story barbershop building. My brother got away the same way he always got away. Wheel, my uncle Earnest nicknamed Tyrone, I guess, because

Tyrone knew how to roll like a wagon wheel. Nicknaming, according to *Invisible Man* author Ralph Ellison, is the Black art of escape. I asked myself, sitting there in that paisley chair. I asked myself, am I an escapee, did I get out of Whitetown, out of Hampstead, North Carolina or still, am I just a little, dark complexed boy named *Boy*, catching fish and Venus flytraps?

I thought about train-seat people and train-stop people getting away from somewhere, going somewhere or anywhere or nowhere. I thought about the path of my tracks that led away from and led back to Hampstead, just around the corner from every place I will ever wander to and through. Maybe those Gypsies did kidnap me after all and it's just that I don't quite remember quite how long Gypsy Rose Lee's fingers really were. She said, "Come here, son." Maybe her Gypsy eyes never broke away from the way I now plainly see the designs of paisley. How else is it that I ended up being as Gypsy as any one of them? Kerouac was a Gypsy. The Beatnik movement was a Gypsy movement. The Beatnik movement was the predecessor to the Flower Power movement. The hippies of the 1960s wandered in and out of towns across America just like Gypsies. Maybe those Gypsies did kidnap me. Maybe the Goatman's two black and white goats resting beneath the shade of my George Washington oak tree when I was four or five, staring at me, knew from the beginning that remembered numbers never add up. It's hard to count the influence of insightful, paisley persuasion. "Come here, son," she said. Maybe I came as called, got into the back seat of that snapbean green car between those three beautiful Gypsy little girls, wrapped myself in Gypsy colors and ended up here in San Francisco so many wandering years later.

I thought about people I met along the way, people like the salt shaking man sitting at a table next to me in a breakfast restaurant in Salt Lake City, pouring a salt shaker down his throat, telling me Jack Kerouac didn't live around there as far as he could tell, and I could tell he couldn't tell straight from crooked. I thought about a pair of tight yellow shorts, a street artist girl outside of 30th Street Station in Philadelphia, drawing pictures of tourists, one dollar each. She drew a cartoon picture of me, I gave her five dollars because her shorts were so tight and so yellow. I thought about the Amish people I met on the train ride between Philadelphia and Chicago but did not meet on the train ride between Philadelphia and Chicago because they would not make eye contact. A baby less than 2 years, an Amish baby had already learned not to look at me when I tried to smile at him or her, I couldn't tell. I thought about the palm reading lady sitting in the psychic corner of an upstairs restaurant next door to City Lights Bookstore, 261 Columbus Ave., San Francisco. I walked in and she was just sitting there with her black back out, wearing a low cut white dress. I give her five dollars to read my palm, but I read hers instead. She forgot to give me my money back and I forgot to ask for it. I thought about Junior Boy, a-pretend-to-be homeless Blackman. He told me he sleeps on park benches in the day because he can't sleep at home at night. He woke up when he saw me coming, asked me for a cigarette. I told him I didn't have any, didn't smoke, then he asked for a light. He introduce himself as John Jackson. "People call me Junior Boy," he said. I told him I was looking for Jack Kerouac, I told him Kerouac was dead. I told him Kerouac died in St. Petersburg, Florida in 1969. I told him that Kerouac was buried in the Edson Cemetery in Lowell, Massachusetts. Stunned and scattered that I was looking for a dead man, John Jackson Jr. was dead serious when he said, "You ain't never gonna find that nigger."

Deep into the deepest part of the evening, deep in the seat of that paisley chair, I thought twice about Spencer. I thought about his golf clubs and his "Everything." And I thought about Fromm. Spencer and Fromm, each cartographers in their own map making way. I thought and I thought and I thought and I remembered when I fell into the night of Allyson. Allyson and me holding hands, running through the Chi-Town night, jumping puddles like teenagers in love, trying to make it to the bus stop before bus #29 decided to pull away. The ghost of somebody beautiful told the beautiful ghost of a storefront mannequin to tell me the story of when my mother danced beautifully with none other than Buddy Guy. The Chicago bluesman, Buddy Guy, took my mother to Las Vegas the same year I was born. He bought my mother a one way ticket back home when he found out she was pregnant with my father's son, me. So that Chicago night, Allyson and I were going to see if Buddy Guy's place was still in the same place it used to want to be when my mother was carrying me and her suitcases. Winded, breathing one breath, we fell into the last seat on a damn near empty bus #29. Allyson took both my hands into hers and said, "You know what, Hudson?" "What?" I said. "You know," she smiled her lipstick look,

"You know maybe you're not looking for Jack Kerouac, maybe Jack Kerouac is looking for you." I don't know how many moments had passed when the beautiful voice I had fallen madly in love with started singing lyrics from a Stevie Nicks song, "When the rain washes you clean, you'll know."

I woke up the next morning still sitting in a paisley colored chair, a Welch witch Stevie Nicks still dancing like a witch at Red Rock in my dreadlocks. My train of thoughts had raced on by only to stop and start red as un-smeared red lipstick. A cold shower, a cold California burrito for breakfast, I packed my Kerouac backpack, checked out of my rented room and walked to a familiar place where over-crowded buses still stop for strangers. I thought about all the buses of my childhood, the Sea Shore Line, the Eastern Shore Line, Miss Lockey's blueberry bus, the Myrtle Beach bus (the chartered bus that took all of us Colored children to North Myrtle Beach every summer because we were not welcomed in the waters of our hometown beaches), the butter bean picking bus, the strawberry fields bus, the Wilmington Transit Authority city bus. I lined them all up in my mind and one by one, pulled the cord, telling each driver, "This is where I get off."

The airport was Sunday-morning-crowded, I guess people love flying on the holiest day of the week. My Jack Kerouac backpack was heavy with thoughts that felt so light when I put it on the checked baggage scale. My boarding pass promised me a window seat. The Golden Gate Bridge is really orange, but in a certain piss-colored light, it appears golden.

So I arrived in San Francisco on a train and left San Francisco on a jet airplane, no more nights on a train for me for a while. No, I did not leave my heart in San Francisco, but San Francisco left its heart in me. Like a Tennessee Williams play, Tom looking for a piece of blue glass menagerie. "No, I did not go to the moon, I went much farther."

About the Author

A North Carolina native from the rural-backwoods-fishing community of Hampstead, Earl Sherman Braggs is a UC Foundation and Battle Professor of English at the University of Tennessee at Chattanooga. Braggs is the author of thirteen collections of poetry. *Hat Dancing with Miss Bessie Smith* and *Negro Side of the Moon* are his latest. Among his many awards are the Anhinga Poetry Prize, the Cleveland (Ohio) State Poetry Prize (unable to accept, manuscript won in two places at the same time), the C&R Poetry Prize, the Jack Kerouac International Literary Prize, the Knoxville News Sentinel Poetry Award and the Gloucester County Poetry Prize. Braggs' novel, *Looking for Jack Kerouac* was a finalist for the James Jones First Novel Contest. *Cruising Weather Wind Blue* is forthcoming from Anhinga press. *Obama's Children* is forthcoming from Madville Press.

www.ingramcontent.com/pod-product-compliance
Lightning Source LLC
Chambersburg PA
CBHW031123080526
44587CB000118/1090